Editors: Nicola Barber, Thomas Keegan
Designer: Ben White
Consultant: Barbara Taylor
Illustrators: Peter Bull, Kuo Kang Chen

Published in 1990 by Kingfisher Books,
Elsley House, 24–30 Great Titchfield Street,
London W1P 7AD

The material in this book has previously been published
in paperback by Kingfisher Books (1989, 1990)
in four separate volumes – Fun with Science:
Sound, Electricity and Magnets, Simple Chemistry, Weather

Reprinted 1991, 1993

© Grisewood and Dempsey Ltd 1989, 1990

BRITISH LIBRARY CATALOGUING IN PUBLICATION DATA

Parker, Steve, 1952–
  More fun with science.
  I. Title   II. Cash, Terry   III. Chen, Kuo Kang
  IV. Bull, Peter
  500

ISBN 0-86272-578-X

Phototypeset by Tradespools Ltd, Frome, Somerset
and Wyvern Typesetting Ltd, Bristol, Avon
Colour separations by Scantrans pte Ltd, Singapore
Printed in Hong Kong by South China Printing Company (1988) Limited

KINGFISHER

MORE FUN WITH

SCIENCE

EXPERIMENTS • TRICKS • THINGS TO MAKE

TERRY CASH & STEVE PARKER

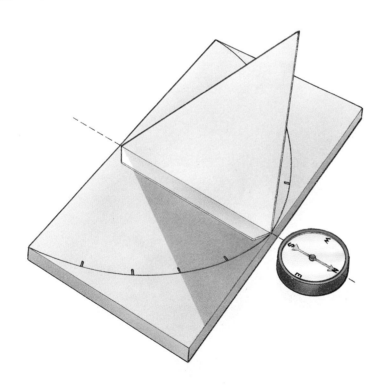

Kingfisher Books

Contents

Simple Chemistry

Weather

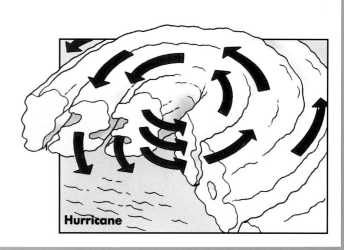

Hurricane

Before you start

This book is full of simple science experiments that will help you to discover more about how things happen in the world around you. The four sections – Electricity and Magnets, Sound, Simple Chemistry and Weather – are each divided into a number of topics. Where a new topic begins, there is a blue line around the page.

You will be able to find most of the equipment you need for your experiments around your home. You do not need expensive equipment to be a good scientist.

A word of warning

Some science experiments can be dangerous. Ask an adult to help you with difficult hammering or cutting and any experiments that involve flames, hot liquids or chemicals. Don't forget to put out any flames and turn off the heat when you have finished. Good scientists avoid accidents.

How to be a good scientist

● Collect all the equipment you need before you start.
● Keep a notebook. Write down what you do in your experiments and what happens.
● Watch your experiments carefully. Sometimes things happen very quickly and you may have to try a test more than once.

● If your experiment does not work properly the first time, try again or try doing it in a different way until you succeed.
● If your answers are not exactly the same as those in the book, do not worry. It does not mean that you are wrong. See if you can work out what has happened and why.

Finding out more

● Make small changes in the design of your equipment to see if the results are still the same.
● Make up your own experiments to test your ideas about how things work.
● Look out for examples of the scientific ideas described in this book around your home and out of doors.
● Do not worry if you do not understand all the things you see – there are always new things to discover. Remember that many of the most famous scientific discoveries were made by accident.

SOUND

This section of the book will help you to investigate sound. Think about sound when you listen to music or when you hear an aeroplane passing overhead.

There are six main topics in this section:

- What is sound?
- Hearing sounds, echoes, acoustics, noise
- The speed of sound
- Music from strings or pipes; pitch
- Percussion instruments; recorded music
- Animal sound

Use the symbols below to help you identify the three kinds of practical activities in this book.

EXPERIMENTS

TRICKS

THINGS TO MAKE

Introduction

Sit still, close your eyes and listen. Sounds are all around you. Even on the quietest night there are sounds such as distant traffic, rustling leaves or the sound of your own heart beating. Which of the sounds are natural sounds, made by animals, trees, people or the wind? Which of the sounds are made by machines working? Are the sounds loud, noisy, quiet or musical?

The experiments in the first part of this section will help you to discover how sounds are made and how our ears help us to hear sounds. In the second half of this section, you can investigate how musical instruments produce sounds and find out how to make a variety of simple instruments, such as drums, an elastic band guitar, a glass xylophone, tubular bells, a packing case bass and a one-string banjo.

The questions on these two pages are based on the scientific ideas explained in this section. As you carry out the experiments, you will be able to answer these questions and understand more about sounds in the world around you.

▲ Why do sound waves from a tuning fork make the water splash? (page 15)

▼ Why do we hear a sonic boom when Concorde flies overhead? (page 27)

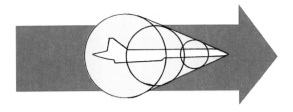

▼ How are echoes used to detect shoals of fish? (page 23)

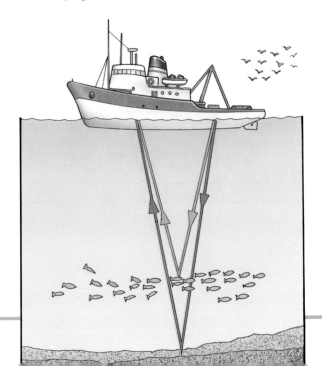

▶ How does the size of a drum affect the sound it makes? (page 41)

▲ Do long pipes make higher notes or lower notes than the short pipes? (page 37)

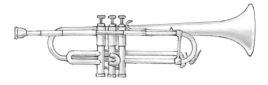

▼ How do our ears filter out unwanted noises? (page 24)

▲ Why does a trumpet player need to 'blow raspberries' (page 36)

▼ On this elastic band guitar, do the tightly stretched bands make high notes or low notes? (page 35)

▲ How can you vary the pitch of the notes made by twanging a ruler? (page 30)

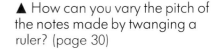

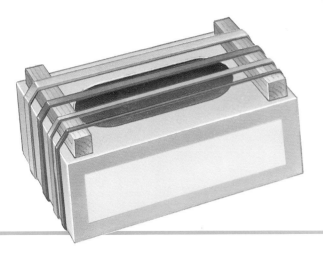

▶ Why does the sound made by the siren of a moving vehicle drop to a lower note as the vehicle passes you? (page 26)

Making Sounds

From singing and stamping to clapping and clicking your fingers, you can make all sorts of sounds with different parts of your body. Try copying the sounds of animals or objects such as a clock or a car. How many different sounds can you make?

▶ Ventriloquists can use their own voices to make a model of a person or an animal look as if it is speaking. To do this, ventriloquists have to learn how to speak without moving their lips. You can try this yourself, but it takes a lot of practice.

Whistle, Hoot or Pop

Whistle
Loud whistles are made with your fingers and lips. Curl your tongue back slightly and place the first and second fingers of each hand into your mouth so that the tips of your second fingers just touch together underneath your tongue.

Now blow through the small gap between your lips and your fingers. You will feel the air rushing out between your lips and, with practice, you should produce a whistling sound.

Hoot
To hoot like an owl, cup your hands together with your thumbs side by side. Make a little gap between your thumbs and blow gently across the hole – not straight into it. It will take some practice to get this right, but keep trying.

Snap
and Click

Can you snap your fingers? First push your thumb and middle finger together. Keep pushing, but slide your thumb to one side so that your middle finger snaps down into your palm with a loud click. It helps if your fingers are slightly damp. With practice you should be able to snap two fingers at the same time.

More things to try

- When people are frightened, they say their knees 'knock'. Can you 'knock' your knees together to make a sound?
- Do your teeth 'chatter' when you are cold?
- Beat your chest like a drum. Then do the same thing while you shout "Aaahh!". How does the sound change?

Pop

Have you heard a cork being pulled from a bottle? If it is pulled out quickly, air suddenly rushes into the neck of the bottle and makes a loud, popping sound.

To make the same sound, put your first finger into your mouth and make a small, round 'O' shape with your lips. Press the pad of your fingertip against the inside of your cheek and flick it firmly out of your mouth.

▲ In the Spanish dance called flamenco the dancer clicks her fingers above her head in time with the music. Sometimes castanets are held in the hands and used to make the clicking sounds.

Shaking the Air

All things which make a sound have one thing in common – they make the air shake back and forth very fast. These shaking movements are called **vibrations**. If the vibrations reach our ears, we 'hear' the sound – *see pages 16–17*.

Sound Waves

A sound makes tiny particles (molecules) in the air bump into each other. When this happens, the molecules are first squashed together, and then expand again, so passing on their energy to the molecules next to them. Individual molecules vibrate slightly to and fro but do not move through the air. The vibrations passing from molecule to molecule are what we call **sound waves**.

You can see how this works by using a row of marbles to represent molecules in the air.

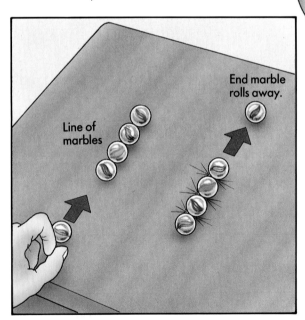

End marble rolls away.

Line of marbles

Arrange four marbles in a line. Then flick a fifth marble so it hits one end of the line. One by one, each marble will hit the next one and pass energy along the line. When the fourth marble receives the energy, it will roll away.

Seeing Vibrations

Put a few grains of rice on a drum skin and tap the skin gently. The vibrations of the drum skin, stretched tight over the frame, will make the rice dance and jump. If you tap the skin harder, what happens to the rice?

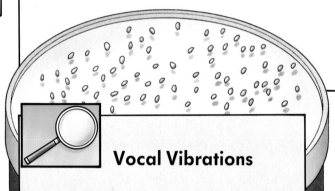

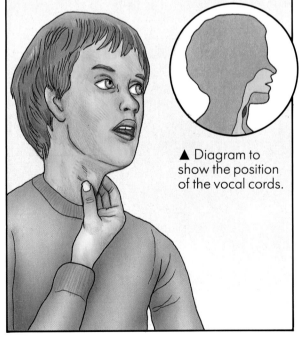

Vocal Vibrations

Hold your fingers against your throat while you speak. Can you feel the sound? When you speak, shout or sing, air is pushed from your lungs over flaps of muscle called **vocal cords**, which are at the top of your windpipe. The air rushing over your vocal cords makes them vibrate and this generates the sound of your voice. Women have higher voices than men because their vocal cords are shorter and more tightly stretched.

▲ Diagram to show the position of the vocal cords.

You can also see vibrations with a tuning fork and a glass of water.

Tap the tuning fork on the palm of your hand and hold the fork in some water in a glass. Can you see how the vibrations of the fork make the water shake?

Hint
After this investigation, dry the tuning fork thoroughly.

Make a Sound Cannon

This trick shows you how to blow out a candle with sound waves.

Equipment: A cardboard tube, some thin, clinging plastic wrap or pieces cut from a plastic bag, scissors, sticky tape, a small candle, a saucer or dish, sand or soil.

1. Cover both ends of the tube with clinging plastic wrap or tape a piece of plastic tightly across each end.
2. Use the scissors to make a small hole in the plastic at one end of the tube.
3. Put some sand or soil in the saucer or dish and stand a small birthday-cake candle in the sand or soil.
4. Ask an adult to light the candle for you.
5. Hold the end of your 'sound cannon' with the hole in it about 2–3 cm (1 inch) away from the candle flame.
6. When you tap the other end of the tube with your finger, the flame should go out.

How it works
It will sound as if you have tapped a small drum. The vibrations from the plastic drum skin will push the air inside the tube out through the small hole in the plastic with enough force to blow out the candle.

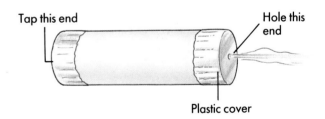

Tap this end

Hole this end

Plastic cover

Sand or soil to hold candle steady.

Hearing Sounds

The next six pages will help you to understand how our ears enable us to hear the sounds around us.

Looking at the Ear

The ear is an amazing and complex part of the body. The bit that sticks out of the side of your head, the outer ear, is only part of the ear. The rest of the ear is inside your head.

The outer ear
The outer ear is shaped like a funnel to collect sounds and direct them inside your head. The sounds, in the form of vibrating air, hit a thin sheet of skin called the **eardrum** and make it shake.

The middle ear
Here, three tiny bones, the **hammer** (malleus), the **anvil** (incus), and the **stirrup** (stapes), increase (amplify) the vibrations from the eardrum and pass them on to the inner ear.

The inner ear
In the inner ear, a shell-shaped organ called the **cochlea** changes the vibrations into electrical messages. These messages are carried to the brain along nerves. The brain interprets the messages it receives and we 'hear' the sounds.

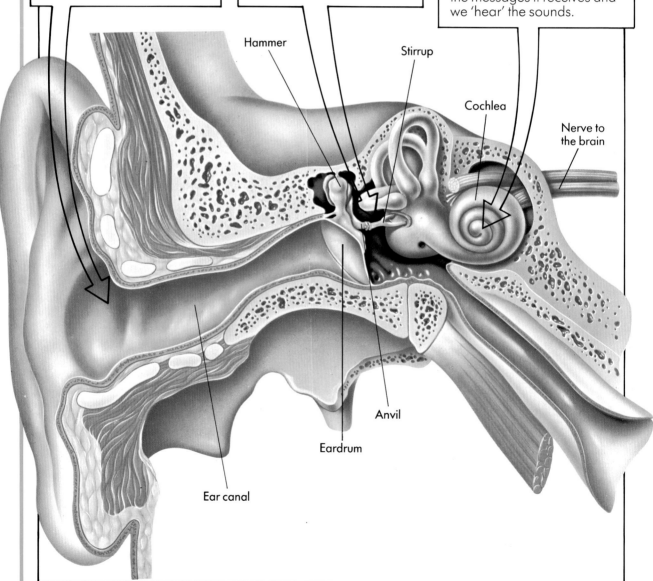

Hammer

Stirrup

Cochlea

Nerve to the brain

Anvil

Eardrum

Ear canal

How Good is Your Hearing?

Equipment: A tiny object such as a pin, a ruler, notebook and pencil.

Ask a friend to help you with this experiment.
1. Ask your friend to stand with his back to the table.
2. Drop the pin on to the table from a height of about 10 cm (4 inches). Make sure you drop the pin from the same height each time – check the height with the ruler.
3. Ask your friend to put up his hand if he can hear the pin hitting the table.
4. Measure the distance from the table to your friend and make a note of the distance.
5. Then ask your friend to take two steps further away and repeat the experiment until he can no longer hear the pin drop.
6. Try the same experiment on some other friends and compare your results.

Drop pin from same height each time.

Where is the Sound Coming From?

We can usually tell where a sound is coming from. To tell the direction of a sound, we turn the head until the sound can be heard equally strongly with both ears.

Many other animals, such as horses and rabbits, can swivel their long ears in many directions. This helps them to sense danger, such as the approach of an enemy.

Ask some friends to help you test how good our ears are at telling the direction of a sound.

Blindfold a volunteer and stand in a ring around him or her. Take turns to make a gentle noise, such as a clap of hands, a click of the fingers or a quiet call. After each sound, the person with the blindfold should point to where they think the sound is coming from. How good are they at pin-pointing the direction?

Then try the same experiment with an ear muff or a pad of cotton wool over one of the person's ears. Does this make their sense of direction better or worse?

Blindfold

Making Sounds Louder

Most of us are able to hear well. But as we grow older, our hearing usually becomes less sensitive, and some people may also experience temporary or permanent deafness as a result of disease.

Some people with hearing problems can be helped by wearing a hearing aid. This is a miniature electrical amplifier which is fitted behind or inside the ear. It makes sounds much louder and passes them straight into the ear canal.

▶ A megaphone is used when a person is speaking to a large crowd of people, in order to increase the sound of their voice.

Make an Ear Trumpet

Roll a large sheet of paper or card into a cone shape and tape the ends to hold them in place. The cone should be as wide as possible at one end and narrow enough at the other end to fit comfortably into your ear.

When you put the ear trumpet to your ear, notice how much louder sounds appear to be. If you point the trumpet towards a quiet sound on the other side of a room, you should be able to hear the sound clearly.

By turning the trumpet around and shouting into the narrow end, you can make your voice sound louder.

How it works
The trumpet collects sounds and directs them into your ear canal, so you can hear more easily. When you shout into the trumpet, it concentrates the sound energy and stops it from being lost so quickly. This is why your voice sounds louder.

Tick-tock Trick

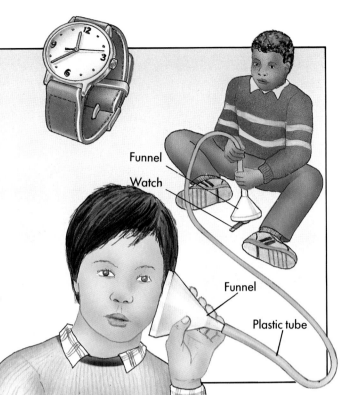

Funnel
Watch
Funnel
Plastic tube

Equipment: Two plastic funnels, about 2 metres (6 feet) of plastic tubing, a mechanical watch or clock (not a digital one).

1. Push one funnel into either end of the tubing.
2. Place the watch on the floor about 2 metres (6 feet) away.
3. Ask a friend to hold one of the funnels over the watch and put the other funnel to your ear. You should be able to hear the watch ticking quite clearly.
4. Experiment with other quiet sounds.

Make a Tube Telephone

You can use the funnels and plastic tubing to make a telephone. It is more fun if you have a long piece of tubing; tape several pieces of tubing together if necessary.

Warning
Don't shout. You could damage your hearing.

Give one end of the telephone to a friend and take the other end into another room. Take it in turns to whisper messages to one another.

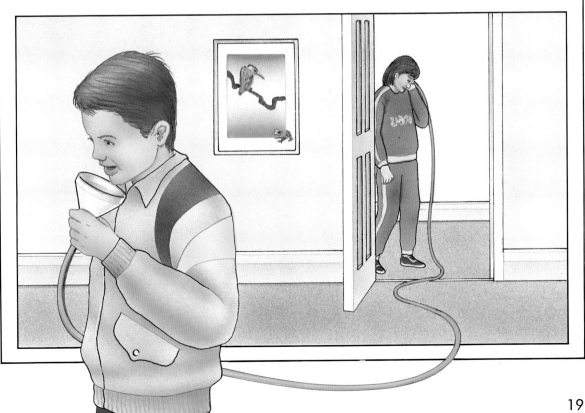

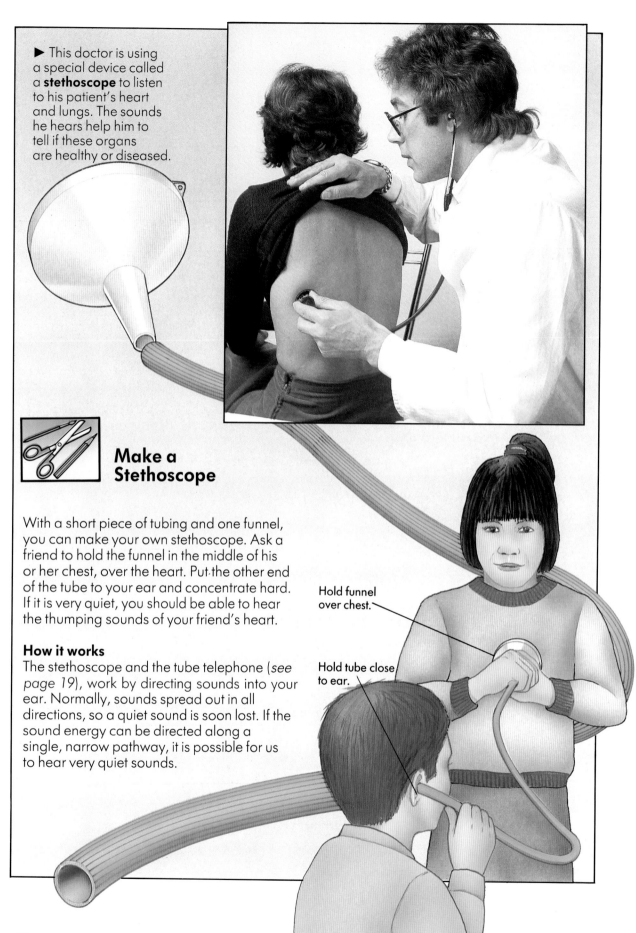

▶ This doctor is using a special device called a **stethoscope** to listen to his patient's heart and lungs. The sounds he hears help him to tell if these organs are healthy or diseased.

Make a Stethoscope

With a short piece of tubing and one funnel, you can make your own stethoscope. Ask a friend to hold the funnel in the middle of his or her chest, over the heart. Put the other end of the tube to your ear and concentrate hard. If it is very quiet, you should be able to hear the thumping sounds of your friend's heart.

How it works
The stethoscope and the tube telephone (*see page 19*), work by directing sounds into your ear. Normally, sounds spread out in all directions, so a quiet sound is soon lost. If the sound energy can be directed along a single, narrow pathway, it is possible for us to hear very quiet sounds.

Hold funnel over chest.

Hold tube close to ear.

Make a Yogurt Pot Telephone

A yogurt pot telephone works in a different way from a tube telephone, but it still uses the vibrations from your voice.

Equipment: Two yogurt pots, string, scissors.

1. Use the scissors to make a hole in the bottom of each pot.
2. Push one end of the string through the hole in one pot and the other end through the hole in the other pot. Knot the string to stop it pulling out of the holes.
3. To use your telephone, stand facing a friend and pull the string tight.
4. Hold your pot to your ear while your friend talks slowly and clearly into the other pot.

Keep the string tight.

Knot in string

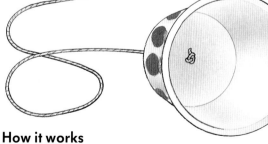

How it works
The vibrations of your friend's voice make their pot shake. The pot makes the string shake and the string passes the vibrations on to your pot. You hear the vibrations as your friend's voice. Why does a yogurt pot telephone work only if the string is held straight and tight?

21

Sound Reflections

When sound waves hit a barrier, such as a cliff, they bounce back and we hear the sound again. This reflected sound is called an **echo**. Out in an open space, an echo is fainter because the vibrations spread out in all directions and lose energy. But in an enclosed space, such as a tunnel, the reflected sound cannot escape and the echoes are very loud.

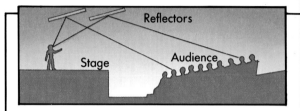

Echoes and Acoustics

Acoustics is the study of how the quality of sound is affected by the shape of a room and the materials it is made from. Acoustics is important in concert halls and theatres where sounds need to be clearly heard.

If there are too many echoes bouncing to and fro between the walls, the audience will hear a confusing jumble of noises. This is called **reverberation**. To reduce the amount of reverberation, a concert hall can be specially shaped and made from materials which absorb sound well, such as wood.

Experiment with Echoes

A good place to find out more about echoes is near a solid wall of rock, such as a cliff. If you face the cliff and shout loudly, the sound of your voice will travel to the cliff and be reflected back at you. If the sound is reflected from different parts of the cliff, you may hear several echoes, as if there were lots of people answering you.

Echoes under the Sea

Echoes can be used to detect shoals of fish, submarines or wrecked ships on the sea bed. Sound waves are sent down into the sea from an instrument called an echo-sounder on board a ship. The time taken for the echoes to bounce back to the ship can be used to work out the position and shape of any objects beneath the ship. It can also be used to map the depth and contours of the sea bed.

This technique is called SONAR – **So**und **N**avigation **a**nd **R**anging. SONAR is so sensitive it can show the difference between one large fish and a shoal of little ones.

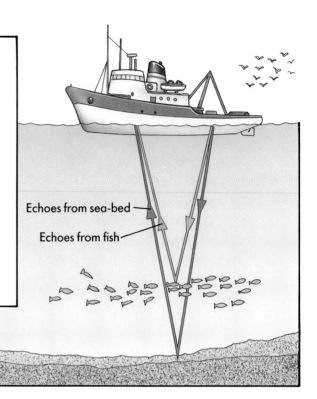

Echoes from sea-bed

Echoes from fish

Animal Echoes

Bats make high squeaking sounds and use their sensitive ears to pick up the echoes from objects around them. The echoes give the bats information about the position and size of objects and help them to work out if objects are moving. This technique is called **echo-location**. It helps bats to find their way in the dark and capture food, such as flying insects.

We cannot hear the echo-squeaks made by bats but we can hear some of the other sounds they make.

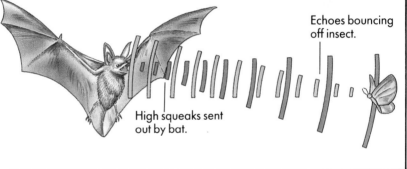

Echoes bouncing off insect.

High squeaks sent out by bat.

▶ A long-eared bat using echo-location to catch a moth for its supper.

Too Much Noise

Sounds which we find unpleasant, we often call **noise**. Noise is made by an irregular pattern of sound waves. Too much noise can damage our hearing and affect body processes such as digestion. It is illegal to make noise above a certain level and some measures (such as fitting cars with silencers) can reduce or prevent noise. But noise pollution is still a serious problem, especially in big cities where vast numbers of people and machines are crowded together.

Measuring Noise

The loudness of a sound can be found by measuring the energy of a sound wave. Loudness is usually measured in **decibels**. A sound of zero decibels is just too faint for the human ear to hear. An ordinary conversation can produce more than 50 decibels of sound energy. In a street full of heavy traffic, the noise is likely to be about 80 decibels or more.

Rustling leaves 10
Whisper 20
Ordinary conversation 40–60
Vacuum cleaner 70
Heavy traffic 90
Pneumatic drill 100
Aircraft engine 100–200
Space rocket 200+

▲ People who use very noisy machines protect their hearing by wearing special ear defenders.

Filtering out Noises

When we are trying to concentrate on a particular task in a noisy place, our hearing system can filter out unwanted sounds.

To see how this works, turn on a tape recorder and read a passage from your favourite book to a friend. After about a minute, stop the tape recorder and ask your friend to tell you what they have just heard. They will remember your reading, but what about any other sounds?

Now turn up the volume and play back the tape. You will be surprised at how many different sounds you can hear in the background. A tape recorder cannot select the sounds it wants to hear in the way we can.

Exploding Bag Trick

Scrunch up the neck of a paper bag and blow into the bag so it puffs up. Hold the neck of the bag tightly and clap the palm of your other hand hard against it. The bag will burst with a loud bang.

The air trapped inside the bag is squashed by your hand and splits through the paper with a lot of force. You hear this as an explosion of sound.

▲ If there are noises near a large accumulation of snow, the vibrations can cause an avalanche. Avalanches are sometimes started deliberately near ski resorts to prevent a dangerous build-up of snow.

Make a Paper Pistol

All you need is a double page from a tabloid newspaper or some brown wrapping paper about 30 cm by 40 cm (12 in by 16 in).

1. Fold the paper in half along the longest side and open it out again.
2. Fold each corner down to meet the line of the centre fold.
3. Fold the paper in half along the centre fold.
4. Fold the paper in half again, press down the crease firmly and open it out again.
5. Fold the widest corners down as shown in the diagram.
6. Fold the paper back to make a triangle shape.
7. To fire your paper pistol, hold it by the long ends and swish it sharply down through the air.

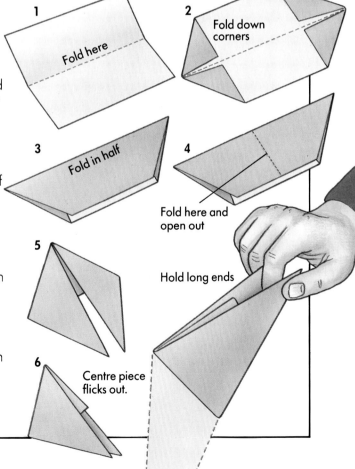

1 Fold here

2 Fold down corners

3 Fold in half

4 Fold here and open out

Hold long ends

5

6 Centre piece flicks out.

The Speed of Sound

A sound does not reach you the instant it is made; it takes time to travel to your ears. This can be difficult to understand unless you actually experience it. For example, if you attend an athletics meeting and sit some distance from the person with the starting gun, you will see the puff of smoke from the gun before you hear the bang. This is because light travels very fast indeed – at about 300,000 kilometres (186,000 miles) in one **second** – while sound travels much more slowly – at a speed of about 330 metres in one second (750 miles in an hour). So you will see the smoke instantly but the sound of the gun will not reach you until later.

Discovering the Speed of Sound

Early experiments to discover the speed of sound were carried out with a gun. A helper with a gun stood a measured distance from an observer with a stopwatch. On a given signal, the helper fired the gun into the air. As soon as the observer saw the flash of flame and smoke from the gun, she started the stopwatch. When she heard the bang from the gun, she stopped the watch. The time between seeing the flash and hearing the bang was the time taken for the sound to travel the measured distance.

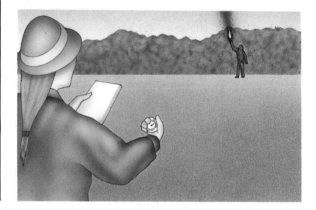

The Doppler Effect

Have you ever noticed that the siren of a moving vehicle seems to drop to a lower note as it passes you? This is due to something called the **Doppler Effect**, which is named after Dr Christian Johann Doppler, who discovered the reason for it in 1842.

Dr Doppler found that if a source of sound is moving, the sound waves are squashed up ahead of it and stretched out behind it. If more sound waves per second reach your ears, you hear higher notes; if fewer sound waves per second reach your ears, you hear lower notes. As a vehicle with its siren blaring passes you, you hear the change from a high to a low note.

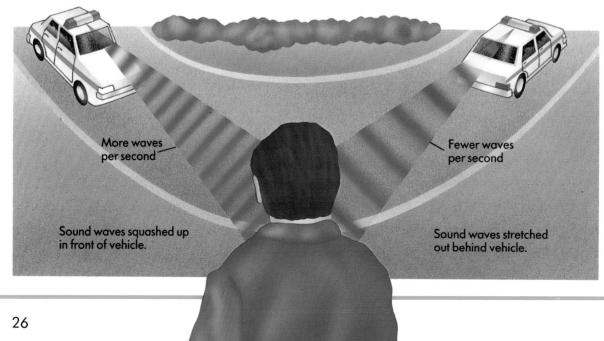

More waves per second

Fewer waves per second

Sound waves squashed up in front of vehicle.

Sound waves stretched out behind vehicle.

Measuring the Speed of Sound

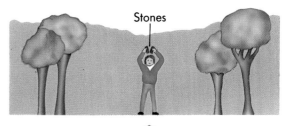

Stones

To measure the speed of sound, you will need a stopwatch and a long tape measure. Measure a distance of 500 metres (1640 feet) as accurately as possible. Ask a friend to stand at one end holding a large stone in each hand while you stand at the other end with the stopwatch. When you shout "Go," your friend should swing his hands together above his head, banging the stones as loudly as possible.

500-metre (1640-feet) distance

As soon as you see the stones clash together, start the watch and as soon as you hear the crack of them hitting each other, stop the watch. Record the time to the nearest tenth of a second. It is a good idea to repeat the experiment a number of times and take an average time.

To work out the speed of sound, use a calculator to divide the distance between you by the time.

Faster than Sound

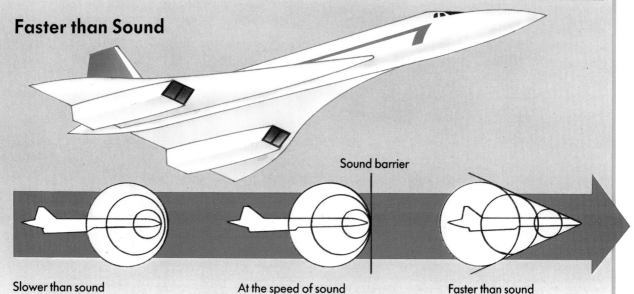

Sound barrier

Slower than sound   At the speed of sound   Faster than sound

A supersonic aircraft, such as Concorde, can fly faster than the speed of sound. As the aircraft approaches the speed of sound, it catches up with the sound waves travelling in front of it and pushes them against each other. This forms a barrier of squashed up (compressed) air in front of the aircraft. As the aircraft reaches the speed of sound, it overtakes this high-pressure air which spreads out behind the aircraft in a powerful 'shock wave'. People on the ground hear the shock wave as a noise like a loud clap of thunder. This is called the **sonic boom** and it has enough force to shatter windows.

Sound on the Move

Sound waves travel at different speeds through different materials. They travel faster through liquids (such as water) and solids (such as steel) than they do through air.

Hearing through Walls

If sounds are being made in a room, the vibrations in the air make the walls and doors vibrate too. Try holding an empty glass against the wall or door nearest to the sound. When you press your ear against the bottom of the glass, the sounds will be much clearer. The vibrating wall or door shakes the air inside the glass and the sounds are passed to your ear.

◄ Out in space there is no air to carry sound vibrations. So when Dr Sally Ride speaks to other astronauts outside the air-pressurized cabin, or Mission Controllers on Earth, she has to use the radio. Radio waves are a type of electro-magnetic radiation and they can travel through space to the Earth.

Listening Underwater

As sound passes about five times faster through water than it does through air, sounds under the water will often seem much louder.

Lie on your back in the bath and keep your mouth and nose above the water but let your ears go under the surface. It will feel very strange at first but, if you listen carefully, your bath water will pass many sounds to you – including the sound of your own breathing. Tap the side of the bath gently and listen to the loud, booming sound that it makes.

Sounds in your Head

Tie some spoons in the middle of a length of string and jingle them together. You will hear a tinkling sound as the spoons knock against one another.

Now press the ends of the string hard against your ears and jingle the spoons again. How is the sound different?

Clench the handle of an ordinary dinner fork tightly between your teeth. Flick the ends of the prongs with your finger and you will hear strange, twanging sounds. Anyone watching you will hear only a faint flicking noise.

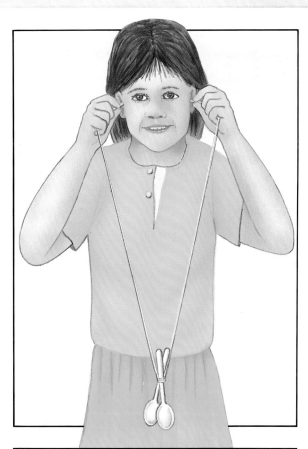

Warning
Do not flick the fork too hard. You might damage your teeth.

How it works
The vibrations from the spoons or the fork pass straight through the bones of your skull to reach your inner ear. The sounds are inside your head and you hear a much louder, deeper sound.

Musical Sounds

In the second half of this book, you can find out about musical sounds, which are made up of a series of notes. You can investigate how different instruments produce high and low notes and change the volume of the sounds they make. By making some simple musical instruments you can discover how string, brass and woodwind instruments produce their own distinctive musical sounds.

Playing the Ruler

Hold a rule on a table with half its length over the edge. Pluck the end of the ruler and listen to the sound.

Now move the ruler so there is only a short length over the edge of the table and pluck it again. Then try the same thing with a long length of ruler over the edge of the table.

As you move the ruler, what happens to the sound? If more of the ruler is over the edge of the table, does the sound become higher or lower?

Sound Boxes

Tap a tuning fork on the palm of your hand and touch the handle of the fork on to a table. What happens to the sound?

How it works
When the tuning fork touches the table, the sound becomes much louder. The vibrations of the fork make the table vibrate too. The table acts like a sound box, passing on its vibrations to the large area of air around it. The table **amplifies** (makes much louder) the sounds made by the fork.

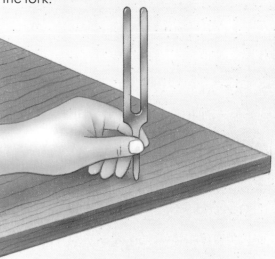

Most musical instruments have something to amplify the sounds they make. In a stringed instrument, such as an ordinary guitar or violin, the strings are stretched across a hollow box, which is usually made from wood. The vibrations of the strings make the wood and the air inside the box vibrate at the same rate as the strings. This is called **resonance**. It makes the sound louder and richer than it would be with the strings alone.

Make a Twanger

Equipment: A wire coat hanger, a pair of pliers or wire cutters, wire staples, a hammer, a block of wood about 15 cm by 10 cm (6 in by 4 in by 2 in).

1. Ask an adult to help you cut the coat hanger into five or six different lengths from 5 to 10 cm (2 to 4 inches) long.
2. Staple the lengths of wire on to the wood block with a hammer.
3. To play the twanger, pluck the wires with your thumbs.

How it works The vibrating wires would not make much sound by themselves but the wood block makes the sound much louder. Do longer lengths of wire make higher or lower notes?

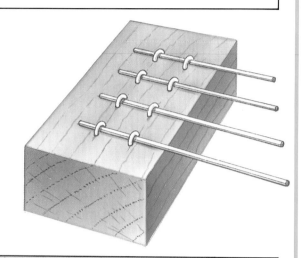

Make a Bull-roarer

You will need a piece of wood about the size of an ordinary ruler. Make a small hole in one end of the wood and tie a piece of string about 150 cm (5 feet) long through the hole.

To make your bull-roarer work, you will need a lot of space, so make sure there is no one standing too close to you. It is a good idea to try this experiment outdoors.

Hold the free end of the string and whirl the wood around your head. As the wood swings around, it makes the air vibrate with a strange roaring noise. Listen to the sound get louder as you swing the roarer faster and faster.

More things to try

Try using a larger, wider piece of wood. You will find that it makes a deeper, louder sound.

High and Low Notes

When musicians talk about the **pitch** of a note, they mean that one note sounds higher or lower than another. There are many different ways of changing the pitch of a note and you will be able to investigate some of them by trying these experiments.

▶ An orchestral xylophone. Each length of wood produces a different note when hit; the longer the wood, the deeper the note.

Underwater Recorder

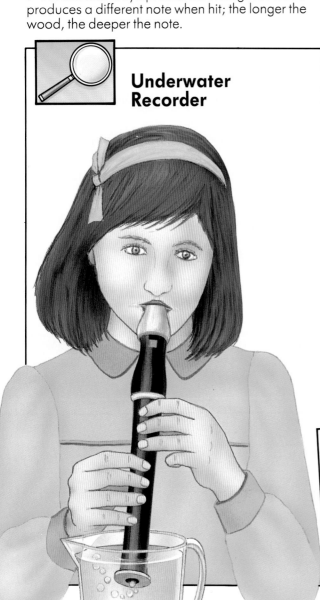

For this experiment, you will need an old, plastic recorder and a tall jug full of water.

Cover all the holes on the recorder with your fingers. (If you find this difficult, stick some tape over the holes.) Blow gently into the recorder and you should hear a single, low-pitched note.

Take a deep breath and blow into the recorder while you push it into the jug of water. What happens to the pitch of the note? Take another breath and blow into the recorder again while you pull it up out of the water. How does the sound change?

How it works
When you blow into the recorder, the air inside it vibrates and you hear a note. The pitch of the note depends on the length of the column of air inside the recorder. When you push the recorder under the water, the water fills up the tube so the column is shorter. You hear a high-pitched note. As you pull the recorder out of the water, the column of air becomes longer and the note sounds lower.

Make a Glass Xylophone

Find four glass beakers which are about the same size and shape. Fill one beaker with water almost to the top. In the second beaker, make the water level come about 2 cm (0.8 inches) from the top of the glass. In the third beaker, make the level 4 cm (1.6 inches) from the top. Don't put any water in the fourth glass.

How to play your xylophone
Tap the side of each glass very gently with a wooden spoon. Each glass will ring with a note of a different pitch. Which glass makes the highest sound and which one makes the lowest sound?

How it works
When you tap each glass, it makes the water in the glass vibrate. The pitch of the note depends on the amount of water in the glass. With more water, the pitch of the note is lower.

More things to try
Try experimenting with different glasses and different amounts of water and see if you can play a tune on your glass xylophone.

Singing Wine Glass

Another way to make music with glass is to rub the edge of a wine glass.

You will need about 2 cm (0.8 inches) of water in the bottom of a wine glass. Hold the base of the glass firmly on the table top with one hand. Wet a finger of the other hand in the water, and rub the wet finger slowly and gently round the rim of the glass.

Experiment by rubbing harder and softer until you find that you can make the glass 'sing' with a clear note. It takes a little practice to get this to work.

More things to try
Try the same experiment with different amounts of water in the glass. How does the pitch of the note change?

Packing Case Bass

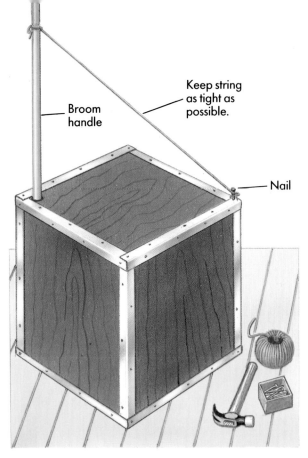

Broom handle

Keep string as tight as possible.

Nail

Equipment: A packing case or large, wooden crate, a broom handle, some string, a nail, a hammer.

1. Ask an adult to help you make a hole in one corner of the bottom of the packing case or crate.
2. Fit the broom handle through the hole.
3. Tie one end of the string tightly to the top of the broom handle.
4. Use the hammer to tap a nail into the lid of the case or crate on the opposite side to the broom handle.
5. Tie the other end of the string round the nail so the string is stretched tight.

How it works
You will produce a rich, deep note because the crate acts like a very large sound box and amplifies the note. If you pull the broom handle back to tighten the string, the pitch of the note will get higher. If you allow the string to become looser, the note will get lower. With practice, you should be able to play simple tunes on your packing case bass.

How to play your bass
Put your foot on the case or crate to hold it steady. Hold the broom handle in one hand and use your other hand to twang the string.

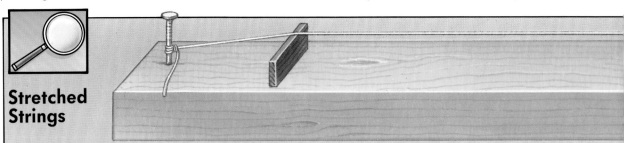

Stretched Strings

This investigation will help you to discover what happens to the sound made by a string when it is stretched.

Equipment: A length of nylon fishing line, a piece of wood about 3 cm (1 inch) thick and 60–90 cm (2–3 feet) long, a nail, a hammer, a small bucket, weights (such as small stones), two small pieces of wood about the size and shape of a thick ice-lolly stick.

1. Bang the nail firmly into one end of the wood.

2. Tie one end of the fishing line to the nail.
3. Place the wood on a table or work surface and pull the fishing line over the wood so it hangs over the side of the table.
4. Tie the bucket to the end of the fishing line.
5. Try to flick the line that is stretched along the wood. You will hear very little because it is rubbing against the wood and cannot vibrate freely.
6. To hold the fishing line above the wood, put a small piece of wood on its side at each end of the line.

Elastic Band Guitar

You can discover more about the effect of tight or slack strings by making this simple instrument.

Equipment: Several elastic bands of various lengths and thicknesses, a cardboard box (such as a shoe-box or a tissue box), scissors, 2 pieces of wood about 1 cm (0.4 inches) square and as wide as the box.

If you have a tissue box, it will probably already have a hole in the top. If you have an ordinary box, use the scissors to cut a hole in the top of the box.

Stretch the elastic bands across the top of the box leaving a gap of about 1 cm (0.4 inches) between each one. If you try to twang the bands, you will find that the sound is rather dull. The vibrations of the bands are muffled because they are rubbing against the top of the box.

If you look closely at a stringed instrument, such as a guitar, you will notice that the strings do not touch the body of the instrument. They are held above it by a piece of wood called the **bridge**.

Use the two pieces of wood to make a bridge for your guitar. When you twang the bands now, the sound will be much clearer. Is the pitch of the notes made by the looser bands higher

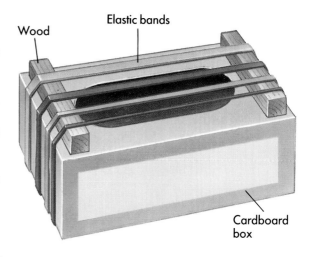

Wood Elastic bands

Cardboard box

or lower than the notes made by the tightly-stretched bands? Experiment until you can play simple tunes on your elastic band guitar.

7. Now twang the line and listen to the note.
8. Put a few weights into the bucket and twang the line again. How does the pitch of the note change?
9. Add several more weights and flick the line again. Is the pitch going up or down?

More things to try
Keep the weights in the bucket the same but move the two supporting sticks closer together and twang the line again. As the length of string between the sticks gets shorter, the pitch of the note will get higher.

Warning
Be careful to keep your feet well away from the bucket in case the line snaps.

Music from Pipes

Instruments which musicians blow into to make musical sounds are made from wooden or metal pipes. The pipes produce a sound when the air inside them is made to vibrate. If the instrument is made from one very long piece of pipe, the pipe may be curled round in a circle or loop.

Instruments such as clarinets or oboes, in which the pipes are made from wood, are called **woodwind instruments**. Brass metal pipes are often used to make trumpets or trombones. These are called **brass instruments**.

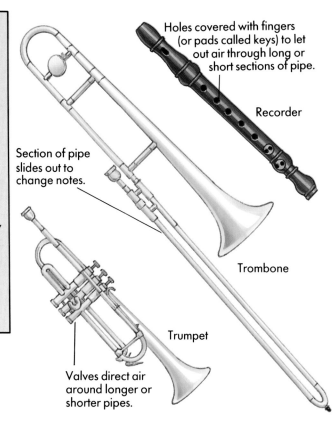

Holes covered with fingers (or pads called keys) to let out air through long or short sections of pipe.

Recorder

Section of pipe slides out to change notes.

Trombone

Trumpet

Valves direct air around longer or shorter pipes.

Bottle Music

All you need are five bottles of the same size and shape and some water.

Fill one bottle with water almost to the top. Fill the second bottle about three-quarters full, the third half full, the fourth a quarter full and leave the last bottle empty. To make the levels easier to see, you could colour the water with a few drops of ink or food colouring. Now try blowing across the top of each bottle.

How it works
When you blow across the top of each bottle, it makes the air inside the bottle vibrate. Small air spaces vibrate more rapidly than large air spaces. When there is very little air in the bottle, you produce a high note. When there is more air, the note is lower.

More things to try
Try the same experiment with different-sized bottles and different levels of water. How many notes can you make?

Blow across top of bottle.

Pipes of Pan

An instrument called Pan's pipes has been used for thousands of years in many different parts of the world.

Equipment: Several pieces of bamboo or hollow plastic piping, modelling clay, sticky tape, scissors.

1. Ask an adult to help you cut the pipes into different lengths so you have a range of lengths between 5 and 20 cm (2 and 8 inches).

2. Push a piece of modelling clay into the end of each tube or seal the end with sticky tape.

3. Arrange the pipes in order of length with the shortest pipe at one end and the longest pipe at the other end. Tape the pipes together so the open ends are exactly level with each other.

4. To play your Pan's pipes, place the edge of the open end of the pipe against your lower lip and blow gently across the top of the pipe.

5. What do you notice about the pitch of the notes from the different pipes?

▲ Chipaya Indians in Bolivia, South America, playing Pan pipes called *zamponas*.

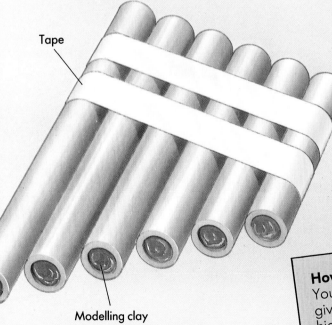

Tape

Modelling clay

How it works

You should discover that the longer pipes give lower notes and the shorter pipes make higher-pitched notes. With a little practice, you will be able to play tunes.

Reeds and Raspberries

Some woodwind instruments use **reeds** to make their musical sounds. When air is blown into the mouthpiece of these instruments, it makes the reeds vibrate, which in turn makes the air inside the pipe vibrate.

Brass instruments do not have reeds in the mouthpiece. Instead the musicians 'blow raspberries' to make their lips vibrate like reeds.

Make a Grass Squawker

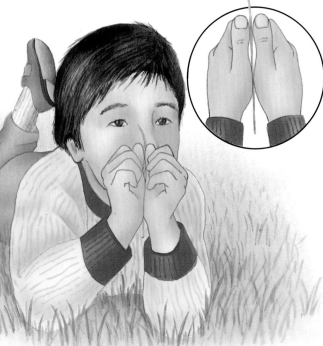

You can make a simple reed from a blade of grass. Choose a large blade of grass and hold it tightly between your thumbs and the heels of your hands.

Now blow hard between your thumbs over the edge of the grass blade. The grass will vibrate with a loud, squawking sound.

Make a Straw Reed

Another form of reed can be made from an ordinary drinking straw. Flatten the end of the straw and cut off the corners to match the diagram below.

Hold the cut end lightly between your lips and blow gently. As you blow, you force air between the straw 'reed' and make it vibrate. The vibrations of the reed make all the air in the straw vibrate in a certain way.

Flatten end of straw.

Cut off ends like this.

More things to try
- Snip off half the straw. Does this make the sound higher or lower?
- In the middle of the straw, make a small cut like this.

Bend the straw up and down to vary the length of the column of air and change the notes.

Playing a Pipe

To see how brass instruments are played, find a piece of old piping about 1 metre (3 feet) long. Purse your lips to make a 'raspberry' sound and blow steadily down the pipe. To make different notes, press your lips more or less tightly together. This is how a bugle player plays simple bugle calls without using keys or valves to change the length of the column of air in the tube.

▶ Brass instruments are played in a different way from woodwind instruments. This trumpet player has to hold his lips tightly against the mouthpiece and 'blow a raspberry'. This makes his lips vibrate like a pair of reeds and sets off vibrations of the air inside the trumpet, which then produces musical sounds.

Shake, Rattle and Roll

For thousands of years, musicians throughout the world have made rhythm instruments, such as drums, shakers, blocks, bells and gongs. Anything that makes an interesting sound when it is hit or shaken can be used as an instrument. Instruments which are played like this are called **percussion instruments**. Many of these instruments can produce notes of only one pitch.

What is in the Box?

This game will test your friends' powers of hearing and detective work.

Equipment: Several small boxes or pots with tightly-fitting lids and a collection of small objects, such as paper clips, small pebbles, buttons, cotton-wool, marbles, polystyrene beads, dried peas, rice and drawing pins.

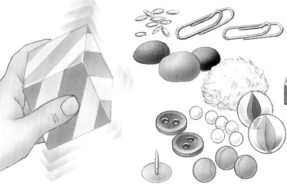

Put each kind of object into a different box and fit on the lid. Ask a friend to shake each box in turn. Then tell your friend that they are allowed to ask up to five questions about the contents of each box. You can only answer "Yes" or "No" to each question. See if your friend can guess what is inside each box.

Make a Shaker

Any empty plastic bottle can be used to make a shaker. You will also need a handful of objects such as small stones, dried peas, uncooked rice, conkers, buttons and small nuts and bolts.

Pour a small amount of one of the objects into the bottle and shake the bottle or twist it against the palm of your hand. Then try each of the other objects in turn to see which makes the best sound.
   When you have made a shaker with a sound that you like, tape the top firmly in place and paint the outside of the bottle.

Make a Drum

Equipment: Empty containers such as plastic bowls, cardboard boxes or tubes, plastic carrier bags, strong string, sticky tape, scissors, thin sticks or dowel.

1. Cut down the sides of the carrier bag and open it out to make one large sheet.

2. Place one of your containers on the plastic and cut around it allowing an extra 7–10 cm (3–4 inches) all round.

3. Ask a friend to help you pull the plastic tightly over the top of the container.

4. While your friend keeps the plastic skin stretched tight, tie string around the edge or use tape to keep the plastic in place.

5. To play your drum, tap it with your fingers or hit it gently with the thin sticks or dowel.

More things to try

- Try making drums of different sizes. To make a big bass drum, stretch a plastic bag over a large waste-paper bin. To make a tiny drum, use a small cardboard tube.

- Make the drum skins out of different materials, such a stiff paper, thin card or the rubber from a balloon.

Hint
To make a good sound, the plastic skin must be stretched as tightly as possible, without any wrinkles.

◀ Drummers in Kenya. Drums have been important instruments for thousands of years. They come in all shapes and sizes and can be made from a variety of materials from wood to plastic.

41

Tubular Bells

1. Ask an adult to help you cut the copper piping into 7 pieces. Make the smallest piece 5 cm (2 inches) long and then increase the length by 2.5 cm (1 inch) each time until you reach 20 cm (8 inches).

2. Tie the string or thread tightly round the end of each length of pipe.

3. Hang the pipes from a piece of wood resting across two chairs. Make sure the pipes hang clear of the ground.

Equipment: Many hardware shops sell lengths of copper piping for plumbing. Ask if they have any odd lengths left over or buy a piece about 1 metre (3 feet) long. You will also need thin string or strong thread, scissors, a piece of wood, two chairs, a large nail.

4. To play your pipes, tap them with the nail and listen to the ringing sound that they make. Which pipe makes the lowest note and which makes the highest note?

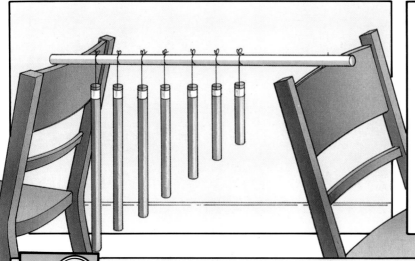

More things to try

Use nails to make a set of chiming bars. Find a nail of every length from about 5 cm (2 inches) to 20 cm (8 inches). Hang up the nails in the same way as the copper piping. Use a nail to play your nail chimes. The longer nails should produce a lower note than the shorter ones.

Playing the Spoons

You can make a very simple rhythm instrument from just two large spoons.

Hold both spoons in one hand with the handle of one spoon between your first and second finger and the handle of the other spoon between your thumb and first finger. Hold the spoons loosely with the bowl of each spoon touching.

When you tap the lower spoon against the palm of your hand, the spoons will hit each other and make a clacking sound. Expert spoon players can tap spoons all over their bodies in time to music. Try this yourself.

Make a Whip Cracker

All you need are two old rulers, some paper, sticky tape and scissors.

Make a pad of paper about 3 cm (1 inch) long and place it between the two rulers at one end. Tape the rulers together around the paper pad. This will hold the rulers slightly apart; there should be a gap of about 0.5 cm (0.2 inches) between them.

To play your whip cracker, hold it by the taped end and hit it against the palm of your hand. It makes a loud crack like a small whip and can be used as another percussion instrument, rather like castanets.

Make a Scraper

All you need are two wooden blocks, sandpaper, scissors, glue, drawing pins.

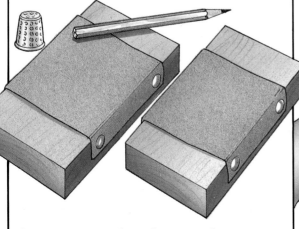

Cut two pieces of sandpaper to fit one side of each wooden block. Glue and pin the sandpaper firmly to the blocks. Hold one block in each hand and rub the sandpaper sides together.

To make other scraping sounds, try rubbing a pencil over one of the pieces of sandpaper. Or put a thimble on one finger and scrape it over the sandpaper.

Balloon Sounds

Blow up a balloon and hold the neck of the balloon between the first fingers and thumbs of both hands. Pull the neck of the balloon into a narrow slit and let the air out slowly.

As the air escapes, it makes the rubber neck of the balloon vibrate, which produces a 'raspberry' noise. Tighten or loosen your hold on the neck of the balloon and see how many different sounds you can make.

Sound and Music

If you make several of the different instruments in the second half of this book, you can form a band with your friends. Make a stringed instrument, a woodwind instrument and percussion instruments. See if you can make up your own music. You could try setting a story to music or make up the sound effects for a play. When you have practised your music, ask an adult to help you record it.

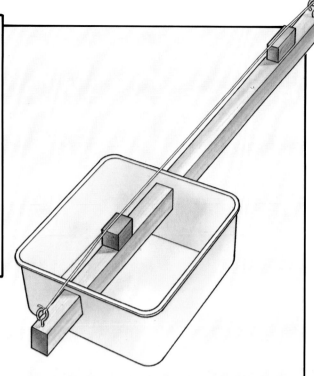

Make a One-string Banjo

Here is another instrument for your band.

1. Use a sharp craft knife to cut two square holes at the front and back of the box just below the lid. The holes need to be big enough for the piece of wood to go through. (Ask an adult to help you with this.)

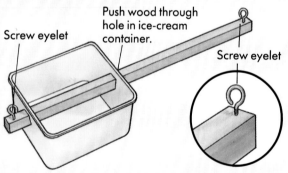

Screw eyelet

Push wood through hole in ice-cream container.

Screw eyelet

2. Push the long piece of wood through both holes so about 5 cm (2 inches) of the wood sticks out of the bottom hole. Glue or tape the wood firmly in place.
3. Screw one eyelet into the top end of the finger board and screw the other eyelet into the bottom end. Tie the fishing line or guitar string tightly between the two eyelets.
4. Use the two small pieces of wood to hold the string above the finger board. Put one piece beside the top eyelet screw and the other across the centre of the ice-cream box.
5. Tighten the string by screwing up the eyelets to take up the slack.
6. Paint your banjo in bright colours.
7. To play your banjo, hold the string tightly against the finger board and strum it gently. To make notes of a different pitch, hold down the string at different points along its length.

Equipment:
• A piece of wood about 90 cm (3 feet) long and 2–3 cm (about 1 inch) square.
• A large, empty ice-cream container with its lid taped firmly in place.
• A piece of fishing line or nylon or wire guitar string about 1 metre (3 feet) long. You will also need two screw eyelets, one for either end of the string.
• Two small pieces of wood to hold the string above the finger board.

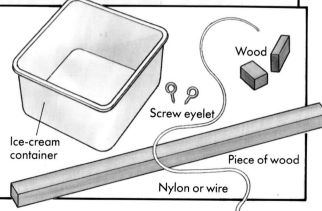

Wood

Screw eyelet

Ice-cream container

Piece of wood

Nylon or wire

Yogurt Pot Record Player

This experiment shows you how sounds are made by records.

You will need an empty yogurt pot and a pin. Use a thimble over the end of your finger or a pair of pliers to push the pin through the middle of the bottom of the pot.

Place the record on the record deck and switch it on. Hold the pot over the record so that the pin rests lightly in the grooves. When you put your ear to the pot, what can you hear?

How it works

The groove in a record is a spiral channel cut in the plastic. At the sides of the channel are tiny lumps and bumps (*see photograph below, right*). When the tip of the needle hits the bumps, it vibrates. The pot acts like a sound box and amplifies the vibrations.

Warning

You must use an old record and ask an adult to help you operate the record deck.

▲ The lumps and bumps in the groove of a record make the needle shake in different patterns of vibrations which we hear as music. This much-enlarged photograph shows a diamond stylus with the grooves of a record behind it.

◄ On an old gramophone like this, the needle fits into the end of a large horn, which (like the yogurt pot) makes the tiny vibrations in the tip of the needle loud enough for people to hear.

Animal Sounds

Animals such as birds, insects, fishes and mammals use sound signals for a variety of purposes, such as to warn others of danger or to attract a mate. The sounds they make carry messages such as ''I live here, keep away,'' or ''Look out, there's an enemy coming''.

Most animals have ears to receive the sounds, although sometimes these are hidden from view. Birds have no outer ear flaps; their slit-like ears are hidden under their feathers. Fish have no outer or middle ear; they hear with part of the inner ear, which reacts to vibrations in the water. Insects have 'ears' in all sorts of unlikely places, such as on their legs or on the side of the abdomen.

Recording Animal Sounds

Try recording animal sounds such as birds singing, bees buzzing around flowers or animals at the zoo. An ordinary radio-cassette recorder works well. If possible, it is a good idea to use a recorder with a manual control for the recording level. A separate microphone is also useful. If you tape the microphone to a stick, it will not pick up sounds made by your fingers.

Before you start to record, make a note of the date, the place and the weather.

Barn owl

Warning Sounds

A grey squirrel makes a single, sharp snort or a ''chuck-chuck charee'' call to warn other squirrels of danger. If the squirrel decides to run away, it waves its tail over its back as it runs as a further warning to its neighbours.

Owl Radar Dish

A barn owl has very sensitive hearing which helps it to hunt for small animals at night. The white disc of feathers on a barn owl's face is an efficient sound collector which works rather like a radar dish.

Singing Whales

We do not know why whales sing, but we know that each whale has a different song. A typical song lasts for about ten minutes and a whale may repeat its song over and over again for 24 hours. Whales may sing to keep in touch with other whales. Sound travels well through water, so whale songs, especially the low notes, may travel for hundreds of miles through the oceans.

Did you know that male mosquitoes are attracted to female mosquitoes by the sound of the females' wingbeats?

Thermometer Cricket

Temperature affects the rate of chirping in grasshoppers and crickets. The Snowy tree cricket has been called the 'thermometer cricket' because it is possible to calculate the temperature in Fahrenheit (very roughly) by adding 40 to the number of chirps it makes in 15 seconds.

▲ A few insects, such as this long-horned grasshopper, have well-developed hearing organs. On both the front legs, just below the 'knee', there are two slit-like openings through which sound enters the 'ears'. The 'ears' contain air sacs which act like sound boxes. Sensory cells on the air sacs respond to vibrations in the air.

▲ In the breeding season, Bullfrogs make loud sounds to attract females and drive other males away. The sounds are made by air being passed to and fro from the mouth to the lungs across the vocal cords. Some of the air enters air sacs in the floor of the mouth which inflate like a balloon and act as a sound box to make the sound louder.

Sound Quiz

1. You always hear things before you see them.

2. Sound travels faster in water than it does in air.

True or False?

3. Which of these guitars will produce the lower note?

Spot the Mistakes

4. What is wrong with these pictures?

5. Mountain avalanches can be started by loud noises.

True or False?

6. Bats use their sharp eyes to spot their prey.

Answers

1. False. Sound travels at 330 metres per second (750 miles per hour) at sea level. Light travels at 300,000 kilometres (186,416 miles) per second, so the light will always reach you first (page 27).

2. True. Water conducts sound waves better than air (page 29).

3. The guitar with the longest string will produce the lower note, the guitar with the shorter string will sound higher (page 34).

4. Top: The ear trumpet is the wrong way round. To amplify sounds the wider end should be pointed towards the source (page 18).
Bottom: The violin needs holes in the body to let out the sound. The body of the instrument vibrates when played and the sound escapes through the holes in the body (page 30).

5. True. Loud noises can dislodge snow from the mountains and cause dangerous avalanches (page 25).

6. False. Bats send out high pitched sound waves and use the echoes to detect their prey (page 23).

48

ELECTRICITY AND MAGNETS

This section of the book will help you to investigate electricity and magnets. Think about electricity when you watch television or speak on the telephone. Think about magnets when you use a compass or an electric motor.

There are seven main topics in this section:

- Static electricity; lightning
- Current electricity; power stations; batteries
- Circuits; conductors and insulators
- Magnetic forces
- Magnetic poles; compasses
- Electro-magnets
- Animals and electricity; electrical machines

Use the symbols below to help you identify the three kinds of practical activities in this book.

EXPERIMENTS

TRICKS

THINGS TO MAKE

Introduction

Without electricity, life as we know it would come to an end. There would be no easy way to make light or heat, to cook our food or keep clean. Think of all the machines in your home or school which need batteries or have to be plugged into an electrical socket to make them work. Yet less than 100 years ago, electricity was a strange, new invention.

The first part of this section will tell you how electricity was first discovered and how it is generated in batteries and power stations. There are plenty of ideas for safe experiments using batteries and bulbs to make circuits and switches. In the second half of this section, you can investigate the mysterious force called magnetism and find out more about the links between electricity and magnetism.

The questions on the opposite page are based on the ideas explained in this section. As you carry out the experiments, you will be able to answer these questions and come to understand the importance of electricity in our world.

Equipment you will need

Many of the experiments in this section use batteries. These are safe to use for experiments with electricity. Here are some of the things you will need:

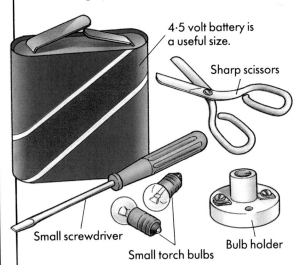

4·5 volt battery is a useful size.

Sharp scissors

Small screwdriver

Small torch bulbs

Bulb holder

How to prepare the wire

Before you use a wire in an experiment, use sharp scissors to strip about 3 cm (1 inch) of the plastic covering from the end. Be careful not to cut through the wires. You need to do this because plastic does not conduct electricity.

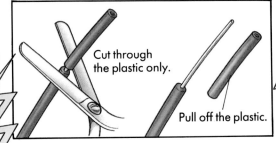

Cut through the plastic only.

Pull off the plastic.

Safety warning
- Never do any experiments with the wires or sockets in your home or school. They are joined to the wires from a power station and the amount of electricity in these wires makes them very dangerous. If you touch a bare wire or a socket which has electricity flowing through it, you will get an electric shock. This can kill you.

- Do not go near electricity pylons, overhead cables or substations. High voltage electricity can jump across a gap and kill you.

◄ How can you make a burglar alarm using a pressure switch? (page 65)

► If one Christmas tree light bulb goes, why do all the other lights go out? (page 63)

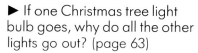

► How can you get electricity from a lemon? (page 61)

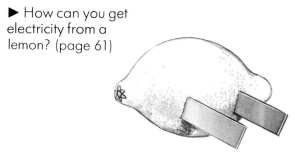

▲ Will this bulb light up if you complete the circuit? (page 62)

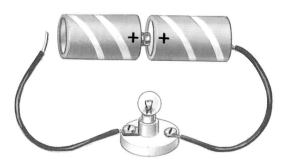

▼ Without any glue, how can you make pieces of paper stick to a comb? (page 52)

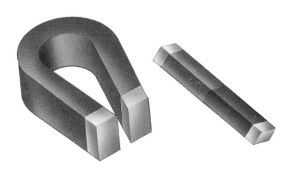

▲ Are horseshoe magnets stronger than bar magnets? (page 73)

▼ Why does lightning often strike tall buildings? (page 57)

▼ How can you make an electro-magnetic crane? (pages 82 and 83)

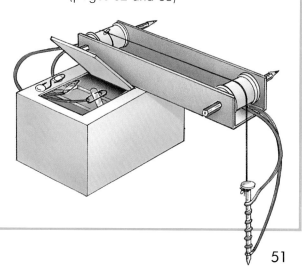

Static Electricity

Electricity was first discovered by the Greeks in about 600BC. A man called Thales found that when he rubbed a piece of amber with some cloth, the amber attracted small objects. (Amber is hardened sap from trees.)

In about AD 1570 an Englishman called William Gilbert carried out similar investigations. He called the effects he saw '**electricity**,' after the Greek word for amber, which is *elektron*. The type of electricity with which Thales and Gilbert experimented is called **static electricity**, which means it does not move.

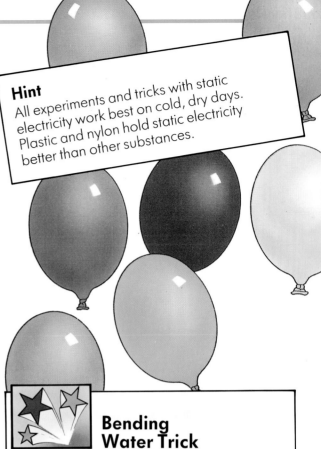

Hint
All experiments and tricks with static electricity work best on cold, dry days. Plastic and nylon hold static electricity better than other substances.

Making Static

You can make static electricity by rubbing things together.

Equipment: A plastic comb, a woollen jumper, tiny scraps of tissue paper.
Rub the comb several times on the woollen jumper. Then hold the comb close to the pieces of tissue paper. What happens to the paper?

How it works
When the comb is rubbed on the jumper, it becomes charged with static electricity and attracts the pieces of paper.

Static charges can be positive or negative. An object with one kind of static charge will attract an object with the opposite charge. In this experiment, the comb has a negative charge and it attracts the paper, which has a positive charge.

Bending Water Trick

Rub a plastic comb to charge it with static electricity and then turn on a tap so the water runs in a thin stream. Hold your charged comb close to the water and watch what happens to the water.

How it works
The water will bend towards the comb because it is attracted by the static electricity in the comb.

Sticky Balloons

This trick shows you how to stick a balloon to the wall without using any glue.

Rub a balloon several times on a woollen jumper and then hold it against a wall. The strong static charge on the plastic skin of the balloon will make it cling to the wall as if it is glued there.

How it works
There is a difference between the charge on the balloon and the charge on the wall, so the balloon is pulled towards the wall. It will stay there until the static charge wears off. How long did your balloon stay on the wall?

The Unfriendly Balloons

If you bring together two objects which have the same kind of static charge, strange things can happen. Ask a friend to help you with this experiment.

1. Tie two balloons together with a piece of thread.

2. Ask your friend to hold a thin stick straight out in front of them. Hang the thread over the stick so the balloons are next to each other.

3. Then rub each balloon long and hard with a woollen jumper.

4. When you let the balloons go, they will try to push each other away.

How it works
When you rub the balloons, you are giving them the same kind of static charge. Things that have the same charge try to push away (**repel**) each other.

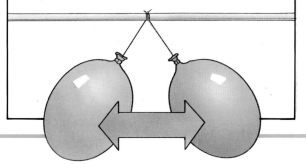

▲ Static electricity can make your hair stand on end! This girl is touching a Van de Graaff generator which gives out a positive charge, making all the hairs on the girl's head have the same static charge. Each hair tries to push away from the next one (because things with the same charge repel), so the girl's hair stands on end.

Rolling Tricks

Equipment: A plastic pen, felt or woollen material, a table tennis ball, plastic drinking straws.

Rub the plastic pen very hard with the felt or wool. Put the table tennis ball on a smooth table top and hold the pen close to the ball. The ball will seem to move at the command of your 'magic wand'. Which way does it roll, towards your wand or away from it?

Now put three plastic straws on the table and arrange them to match the picture. Rub the pen with the felt or wool and hold the side of the pen close to the straw which is on top of others. Can you work out why some things move towards the pen and others move away?

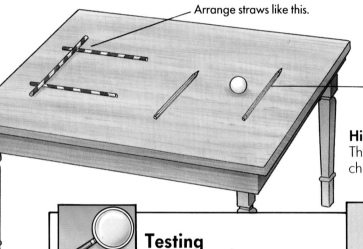

Arrange straws like this.

Hold charged pen close to table tennis ball.

Hint
Think about the two different kinds of static charge – *see pages 52 and 53.*

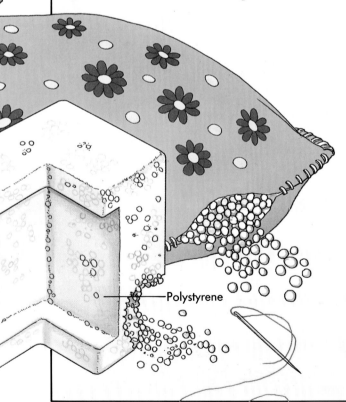

Polystyrene

Testing Static Charges

Equipment: Polystyrene beads, a table tennis ball, felt or woollen material, needle and thread, a collection of objects such as a plastic comb, a plastic pen, a balloon, some clear plastic film, a plastic bag.

1. Find some polystyrene beads (polystyrene is a sort of plastic). You may be able to get a small handful of beads from one of those saggy bags (bean bags) which are used as seats. If not, see if you can find a block of polystyrene (often used as packing) and break off some beads.

2. Thread a piece of cotton through the needle and tie a knot in the end of the thread. Push the needle through the largest polystyrene bead you can find and pull the thread through the hole as far as the knot. Pull the cotton out of the needle and tie it round something so the bead can swing freely.

3. Now rub your collection of objects with the felt or wool. Hold each one in turn close to the polystyrene bead and watch what happens. Make a note of those objects which attract the bead and those which push it away.

4. Repeat the experiment with a table tennis ball hung from a thread. (Use a small piece of tape to attach the thread to the ball.)

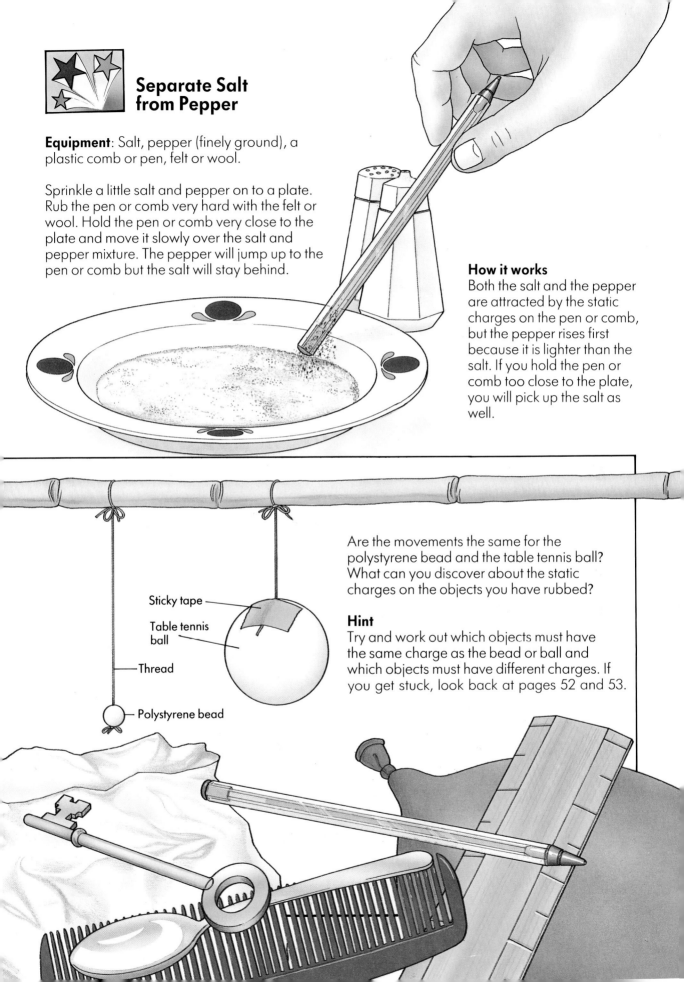

Separate Salt from Pepper

Equipment: Salt, pepper (finely ground), a plastic comb or pen, felt or wool.

Sprinkle a little salt and pepper on to a plate. Rub the pen or comb very hard with the felt or wool. Hold the pen or comb very close to the plate and move it slowly over the salt and pepper mixture. The pepper will jump up to the pen or comb but the salt will stay behind.

How it works
Both the salt and the pepper are attracted by the static charges on the pen or comb, but the pepper rises first because it is lighter than the salt. If you hold the pen or comb too close to the plate, you will pick up the salt as well.

Are the movements the same for the polystyrene bead and the table tennis ball? What can you discover about the static charges on the objects you have rubbed?

Hint
Try and work out which objects must have the same charge as the bead or ball and which objects must have different charges. If you get stuck, look back at pages 52 and 53.

Sticky tape

Table tennis ball

Thread

Polystyrene bead

Electricity in the Sky

Although you may not realize it, you will already have come across one kind of static electricity. This is the powerful 'electricity in the sky' which we call **lightning**.

Crackles and Sparks

Have you ever seen little flashes and sparks of light when you undress in the dark? These sparks are the static electricity which is made by your clothes rubbing together.

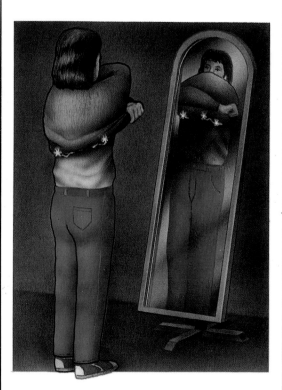

Wear a nylon shirt under a woollen jumper and stand in front of a mirror in a dark room. When you pull off the jumper, you should see the sparks fly.

During a storm, you can see giant sparks of static electricity when lightning flashes across the sky.

Electricity in Clouds

In a storm cloud, the moving air makes tiny water droplets and ice particles rub together so they become charged with static electricity. The positively-charged particles rise to the top of the cloud and the negatively-charged particles sink to the bottom of the cloud.

The negative charges in the cloud are strongly attracted to the ground. They leap from cloud to cloud or from the cloud to the ground as giant flashes of lightning. The lightning makes the air so hot that it explodes with loud booms of thunder.

In 1753, an American scientist, Benjamin Franklin, decided to investigate the charge in storm clouds. He did this in an experiment that was so dangerous he was lucky not to have been killed. **Never even think** of trying the same experiment yourself.

On a stormy day he flew a large kite on a very long line up into a black, mountainous storm cloud. He tied a large iron key to the bottom of his line and when the electrical charge ran down the wet kite line and hit the key, sparks flashed. Luckily he was not hurt and his investigations led to the invention of lightning conductors.

Lightning often strikes the first point it reaches on its journey to the ground, so tall buildings are most likely to be hit. If you look up at church spires and tall buildings, you can sometimes see a metal strip going down the side of the building. This is called a **lightning conductor** and it is usually made of copper.

If lightning strikes the top of the building, electricity will flow safely down the copper strip to the earth instead of damaging the building.

How far is the Storm?

Light travels so quickly (about 300,000 kilometres – 186,416 miles – in one **second**!) that we see a bright flash of lightning instantly. But we have to wait a few moments before we hear the thunder. This is because sound travels much more slowly than light – at only 330 metres in one second (750 miles in an hour).

During a storm, wait until you see a flash of lightning, then start to count slowly. For every count of three, the storm is roughly one kilometre away (a count of five means the storm is about one mile away).

Warning
If you are caught in a thunderstorm do **not** shelter under a tree, especially one that is tall or standing on its own. The lightning may strike the tree and hit you as well.

Electricity on the Move

The electricity we use in our homes and schools is different from static electricity because it moves from place to place. It flows through wires in the same way that water flows through a hose. We call this flow an electric **current**.

Spot the Difference

Can you spot the differences between these two pictures?

In the bottom picture, there are no electric gadgets. Nowadays, we use electricity for so many things it's hard to imagine life without it.

Making Electricity

An electric current was first generated in 1831 by Michael Faraday. He moved a magnet in and out of a coil of wire and found that this made an electric current flow through the wire.

This was a very important discovery which led to the invention of the **dynamo**. Nowadays, we still use dynamos to make almost all our electricity, and much of our present way of life is based on Faraday's discovery.

Testing a Dynamo

On some bicycles, the lights are powered by a simple dynamo. The movement of the wheels makes a magnet turn round inside a coil of wire. This makes electricity flow in the wire and the lights come on.

If you or your friends have a bicycle with a dynamo, try this test. Turn the bicycle upside down and balance it on the handle bars and the saddle. Switch on the front light and turn the pedals slowly at first, then quickly. What happens to the light as the dynamo is turned faster? Why might this be dangerous if you are cycling at night?

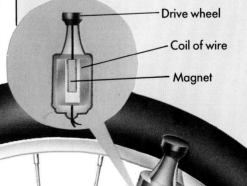

Drive wheel

Coil of wire

Magnet

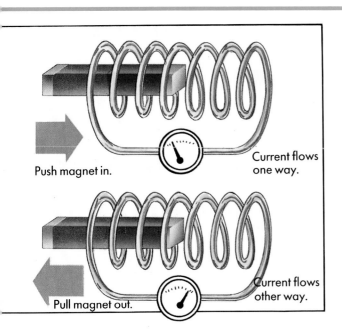

Push magnet in. — Current flows one way.

Pull magnet out. — Current flows other way.

Power Stations

Most of the electricity we use in our homes, schools, shops and factories is made (**generated**) in power stations. In a power station, fuel such as coal or oil is burned to heat water and turn it into steam. The steam pushes a huge wheel, called a **turbine**, round at very high speeds. The turbine turns a massive dynamo called a **generator**, which makes electricity.

From the power station, the electricity is carried along thick wires called **cables** until it reaches our homes or other buildings. The wires may be buried under the ground or they may be hung from tall towers called **pylons**.

To send the electricity over long distances, it first goes through a device called a **transformer**. This increases the voltage of the electricity, (voltage is the pressure which pushes electricity along a wire) and makes it cheaper to move. When the electricity reaches towns or cities, the power is reduced back to the right level for the machines we use by another transformer.

Warning
The electricity in your home is very dangerous; it can easily kill you. **Never** play with plugs, sockets, wires or anything connected to the mains supply.

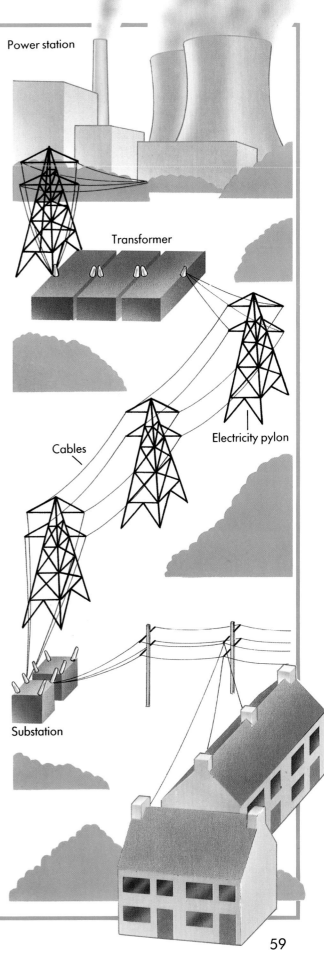

Power station

Transformer

Cables

Electricity pylon

Substation

Battery Power

Even though you must never do experiments with mains electricity, you can discover a lot about electricity in complete safety using small batteries and bulbs. Batteries are useful because they are small enough to be carried from place to place.

▲ Alessandro Volta (*right*) demonstrates his Voltaic pile to Napoleon.

The First Battery

The first battery was made in 1800 by an Italian scientist, Alessandro Volta. Volta discovered that some metals and a liquid could work together to produce electricity.

He made a 'sandwich' of paper soaked in salt water between a piece of silver and a piece of zinc. When he joined the two metals with a wire, he found that a current flowed through the wire. As the current was very weak, he made a pile of his 'sandwiches' and when he touched a wire from the top of the pile to a wire from the bottom, he got sparks of electricity. Volta's battery came to be known as the **Voltaic pile**.

Did you know that the electrical measurement the '**volt**' was named after Volta? The number of volts describes the pressure or '**voltage**' which pushes electricity along a wire.

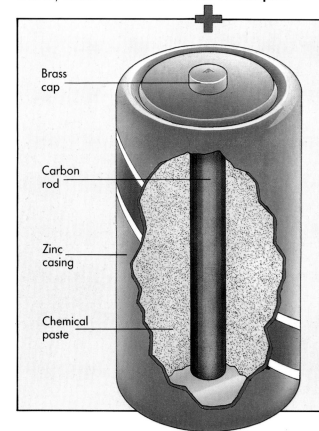

Brass cap

Carbon rod

Zinc casing

Chemical paste

How a Battery Works

The batteries we use today work in a similar way to the battery made by Volta. The case of a battery is made of zinc metal; this is often covered with card and plastic or tin to prevent the battery from leaking. Instead of a piece of silver or copper, there is a carbon rod (rather like a thick pencil lead) in the middle of the battery. The battery case is not filled with salt water because this would easily leak out. Instead, there is a chemical paste between the carbon and the zinc casing.

The chemicals in the battery make electricity. As the electricity is taken from the battery, the chemicals are slowly used up. Eventually, the battery cannot make electricity any more. Some batteries, such as those used in cars, can be recharged so they go on working for longer.

Make your own Battery

Equipment: Two pieces of wire about 30 cm (12 inches) long, sticky tape, 4 copper coins, 4 pieces of zinc, blotting paper soaked in salty water.

1. Sandwich a piece of the salty blotting paper between a coin and a piece of zinc (cut from a battery case).
2. Tape the bare end of one wire to the coin.
3. Now make three more sandwiches.
4. Finally, tape the bare end of the other wire to the piece of zinc on the bottom of your Voltaic pile.
5. Now take the free end of each wire and touch both ends lightly onto your tongue. Can you feel a tingle of electricity?

How it works
In your voltaic pile, chemical reactions cause a tiny electric current. The current flows from one wire, through your tongue and into the other wire. The current is just enough to make your tongue tingle.

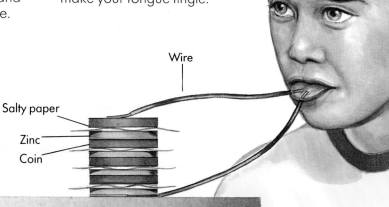

Wire

Salty paper

Zinc

Coin

Can you get Electricity from a Lemon?

Make two slits in the skin of a lemon and push a copper coin into one slit and a piece of zinc into the other slit. Make sure the two metals are not touching each other inside the lemon. If you hold the coin and the zinc gently against your tongue, you should be able to feel a tingle of electricity.

The current flows because a chemical reaction takes place between the metals and an acid in the lemon juice. The lemon juice acts in the same way as Volta's salt water or the chemical paste in the battery.

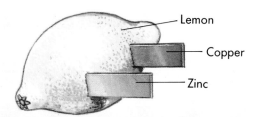

Lemon

Copper

Zinc

put your hands on the plates

▶ At the Launch Pad in the Science Museum, London, the child's slightly damp and salty hands link the two metal plates together and a current flows from one to the other.

Investigating Circuits

To make electricity come out of a battery, you need to give it a path, such as a wire, to move along. Electricity can only move in one direction, so you need to attach a wire from one end (**terminal**) of the battery to the other end. This loop of wire is called a **circuit**. As long as the circuit is complete, electricity will flow. If there is a gap in the circuit, electricity will not be able to flow. It's rather like a toy train on its track. If there are any gaps, the train will not run around the circuit.

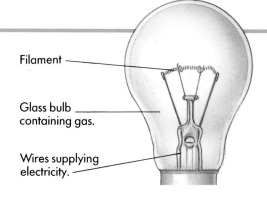

Filament

Glass bulb containing gas.

Wires supplying electricity.

▲ Electricity flows into a light bulb and out again. The wire filament is so thin that the electricity has to push hard to get through the wire. This makes the filament white hot so that it glows with a bright light. The filament is made of a metal called tungsten which can get very hot before it melts. The glass bulb is filled with a gas which helps to stop the filament from burning away too quickly.

Make a Simple Circuit

All you need is a battery, some wire, a small torch bulb and a small bulb holder.

See if you can make the bulb light up. Look carefully at the bulb. Can you see where you need to touch the wires? Don't forget that electricity can only flow if a circuit is complete.

How it works
To make the bulb light up, electricity must flow out of one end of the battery, through the bulb and back to the other end of the battery.
   Inside the bulb, can you see a tiny coiled

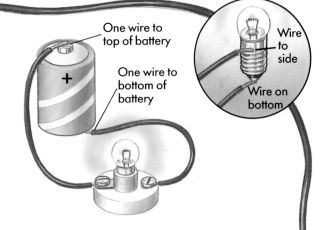

One wire to top of battery

One wire to bottom of battery

Wire to side

Wire on bottom

wire? This is called the **filament**. Electricity can flow through the filament if you touch one wire to the side of the bulb and the other wire to the bottom of the bulb. It is difficult to hold the wires and the bulb together but you can use a bulb holder to do the job for you.

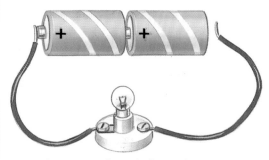

What happens if you link two batteries into your circuit?

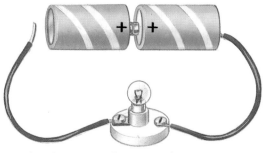

What happens if you put the two negative or the two positive battery ends together?

62

Glowing Wool Trick

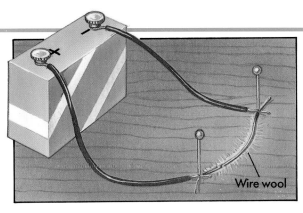

Equipment: A battery, two wires, some steel wool (the kind used for cleaning metal pots and pans).

Pull out one long strand of steel wool and pin it to a board. Attach one wire to one end of the battery and the other wire to the other end. With the free ends of both wires, touch the strand of steel wool. What happens?

Wire wool

How it works
The electrical current flows easily through the wires but has more difficulty passing through the thin strand of steel wool. This makes the steel heat up and glow red hot. With a powerful battery, it may even melt and break.

There are very thin wires in the **fuses** which are fitted into the electrical machines, circuits and plugs in our homes. If something goes wrong with the wiring, the thin fuse wire quickly melts and makes a gap in the circuit. This cuts off the electricity supply and prevents a fire.

Circuit Challenge

Can you link three bulbs to one battery so that all three bulbs light up at the same time? When you have done this, try taking one of the bulbs out of the circuit. Do the other bulbs go out as well?

How it works
There are two different ways of wiring several bulbs into a circuit. One way is to wire up all the bulbs on one circuit. This is called a **series** circuit. The bulbs give out only a dim light because they are all sharing the same power. If you take out one bulb, it breaks the circuit and the other bulbs go out as well.

The other way of wiring up the bulbs is to give each bulb a separate circuit. These are called **parallel** circuits. If you wire up your three bulbs like this, each bulb will look almost as bright as one bulb in a circuit on its own. If you take out one bulb, the other bulbs will all stay on.

▼ Christmas tree lights are wired up in a series circuit. If one bulb goes, all the lights go out.

Series circuit

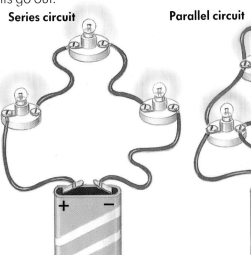

Parallel circuit

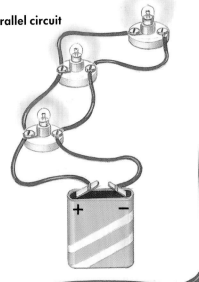

Experiment with Conductors and Insulators

Some materials let electricity flow through them. They are called **conductors**. Other materials stop electricity passing through them. They are called **insulators**. We use conductors to carry electricity to where it is needed and we use insulators to stop it leaking into places where we do not want it to be.

Try this experiment to find out which materials are conductors and which are insulators.

To hold a wire on to a battery terminal, hook it around a paper clip.

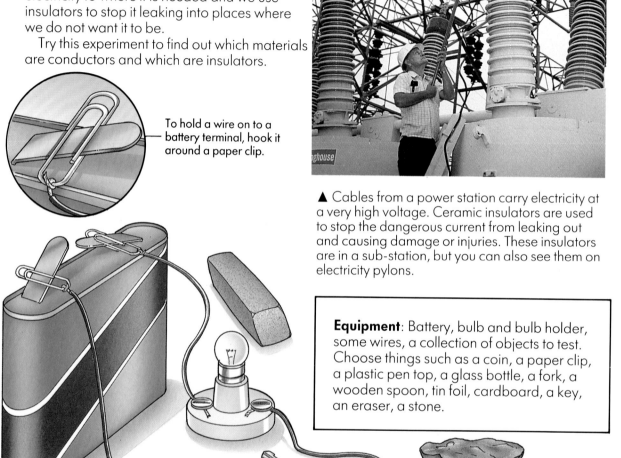

▲ Cables from a power station carry electricity at a very high voltage. Ceramic insulators are used to stop the dangerous current from leaking out and causing damage or injuries. These insulators are in a sub-station, but you can also see them on electricity pylons.

Equipment: Battery, bulb and bulb holder, some wires, a collection of objects to test. Choose things such as a coin, a paper clip, a plastic pen top, a glass bottle, a fork, a wooden spoon, tin foil, cardboard, a key, an eraser, a stone.

1. Make a circuit like the one in the picture.
2. Touch the wires together to make sure the bulb lights up and there are no loose connections.
3. Now touch the ends of both wires to the objects in your collection. Does the bulb light up?

4. Put all the things which made the bulb light up into one pile. These are the conductors. They conduct electricity through themselves and complete the circuit. What are they made from?
5. Put all the things that did not make the bulb light up into another pile. They are insulators. What are the insulators made from?

Bridging the Gap

Equipment: A battery, a bulb and bulb holder, some wires, two metal drawing pins, a metal paper clip, a piece of wood about 8 cm by 5 cm (3 by 2 inches).

A **switch** is a gap in a circuit that can be bridged easily. When a switch is pressed 'on', the gap is closed and the circuit is complete. The electric current can then flow to make a bulb light up or a machine work.

Try making your own switch.
1. Push the drawing pins into the piece of wood. Keep them a little way apart.
2. Trap one wire under one drawing pin and the other wire under the other drawing pin. Join the other ends of the wires to the battery and bulb.
3. Open up the paper clip and hook one end under one drawing pin.
4. To 'switch on', touch the paper clip on to the other drawing pin to complete the circuit.
5. You can 'switch off' the bulb by moving the paper clip away from the drawing pin.

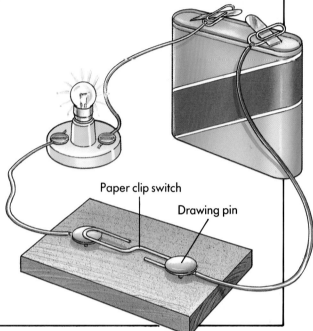

Paper clip switch

Drawing pin

Make a Burglar Alarm

Equipment: A battery, some wires, thin card, tin foil, sticky tape or glue, a small buzzer (from an electrical shop). If you can't get a buzzer, use a bulb in a bulb holder instead.

1. Cut a piece of card about 15 cm by 7.5 cm (6 by 3 inches) and fold it in half.
2. Tape strips of tin foil around the card.

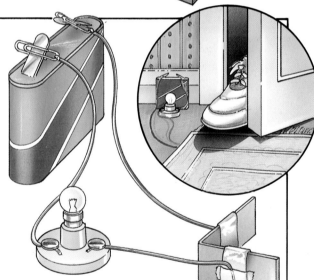

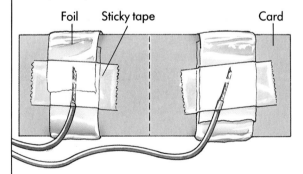

Foil   Sticky tape   Card

3. Tape a wire to each piece of foil.
4. Join the wires into a circuit with the battery and the buzzer or bulb.

5. Set up your burglar alarm near a door so that anyone coming through the door will tread on the card and set off the buzzer or make the bulb light up.

How it works
When the two pieces of foil are pressed together, the circuit is complete and electricity can flow.

Turn on the Light

Try adding lights and switches to a doll's house so you can turn on a light upstairs or downstairs.

Equipment: Large cardboard box, sheets of thin card, paste, glue or sticky tape, 2 bulbs, 2 bulb holders, wire, battery, 4 brass paper fasteners, 2 metal paper clips, doll's house furniture, old pieces of wallpaper and carpet.

1. Make your doll's house from a cardboard box turned on its side. To make a ceiling and some stairs, glue or tape sheets of thin card inside the box.

2. Put the bulbs into the bulb holders and fix two long wires to each holder.

3. Cut a small hole in the ceiling of each room and push the bulbs through the holes.

4. Push the paper fasteners through the side of the box and use the paper clips to make two switches.

5. Connect up the wires to the bulbs, the switches and the battery to make two parallel circuits with a switch on each loop (*see diagram*).

6. Add some decorations and furniture.

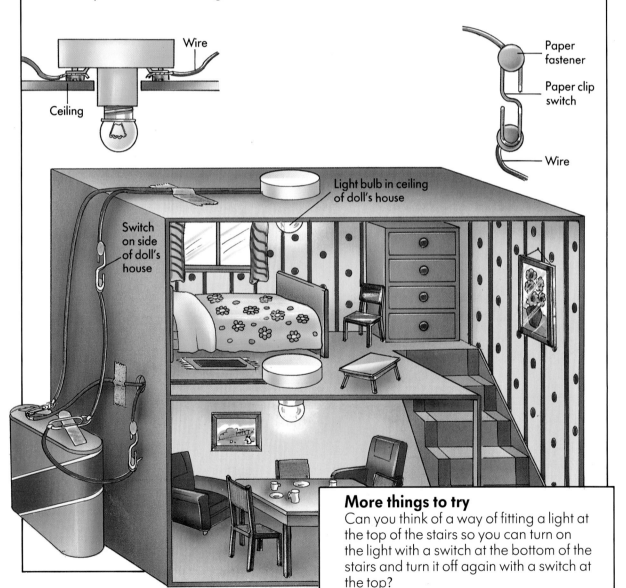

Wire

Ceiling

Paper fastener

Paper clip switch

Wire

Light bulb in ceiling of doll's house

Switch on side of doll's house

More things to try

Can you think of a way of fitting a light at the top of the stairs so you can turn on the light with a switch at the bottom of the stairs and turn it off again with a switch at the top?

Make a Lighthouse

Equipment: An empty washing-up liquid bottle, bulb, bulb holder, battery, wire, scissors, tape, glue, newspaper, paper clip switch, stiff card or wooden board about 20 cm (8 inches) square, thin card, plaster of paris or papier mâché, a clear plastic or glass pot.

1. Pull off the top of the bottle and use the scissors to cut off the bottom of the bottle.

2. Cut two pieces of wire which are both about 15 cm (6 inches) longer than the bottle and join one wire to either side of the bulb holder.

3. Put the bulb into the holder and push the holder up inside the bottle so the bulb comes out of the hole at the top.

4. Tape or glue the bulb holder in place. If you find this difficult, screw up some newspaper and put this inside the bottle to wedge the bulb in place.

5. Glue or tape the plastic or glass pot to the top of the bottle.

6. Make a box out of the thin card and put it (upside down) over the battery.

7. Push some paper fasteners through the top of the box and attach a paper clip to one of the fasteners to make a switch.

8. Join one of the wires from the bulb holder to the switch and the other wire to one of the battery terminals. Join the switch to the other battery terminal with a new piece of wire.

9. Stand the bottle and the box on the thick card or wood.

10. Make up the plaster of paris or the papier mâché and mould it around the bottom of the bottle to make some rocks. Leave a gap around the box so you can lift it up to change the battery.

11. Paint the rocks and the lighthouse.

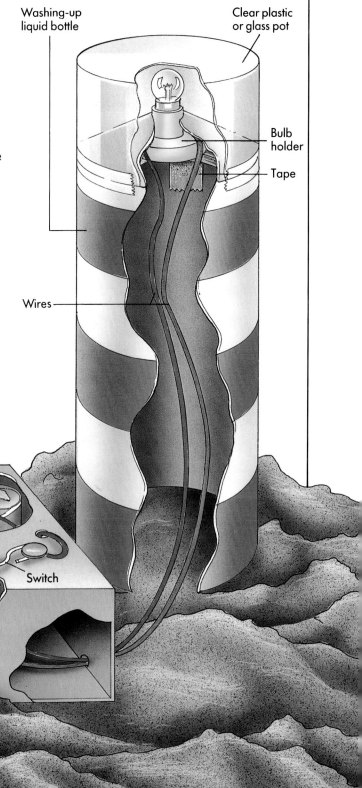

Washing-up liquid bottle

Clear plastic or glass pot

Bulb holder

Tape

Wires

Battery

Cardboard box

Plaster or papier mâché 'rocks'

Switch

Steady Hand Game

Ask an adult to help you make this game.
1. Use the pliers to cut a short piece of wire from the coat hanger. Bend the wire into a loop but leave the end open.
2. Join a short length of wire to the open loop and join the other end of this wire to the bulb holder.
3. With another piece of wire, join the other side of the bulb holder to the battery.
4. Bend the rest of the coat hanger into a long, wavy line.
5. Wind tape round both ends of this wavy line of wire. (When you are not playing the game, you can rest the loop against this tape and the bulb will not light up.)
6. Join one end of the wavy wire to the battery with some wire.
7. Put the wavy wire on to the wooden board and hammer a wire staple over each end of the wire to hold it upright.

Equipment: A block of wood about 50 cm by 20 cm (20 inches by 8 inches), a wire coat hanger, pair of strong pliers, a hammer, wire staples (from a hardware store), battery, bulb in a bulb holder, wire, sticky tape.

8. Bend the end of the open loop around the wavy wire and join up the loop with the pliers.
9. Decorate the board with paints or crayons.
10. Try replacing the bulb with a small buzzer.

How to play the game
Can you or your friends move the loop all the way along the wavy line without making the bulb flash? If your hand shakes, the loop will touch the wire and complete the circuit. Electricity will flow along the wire and the bulb will flash.

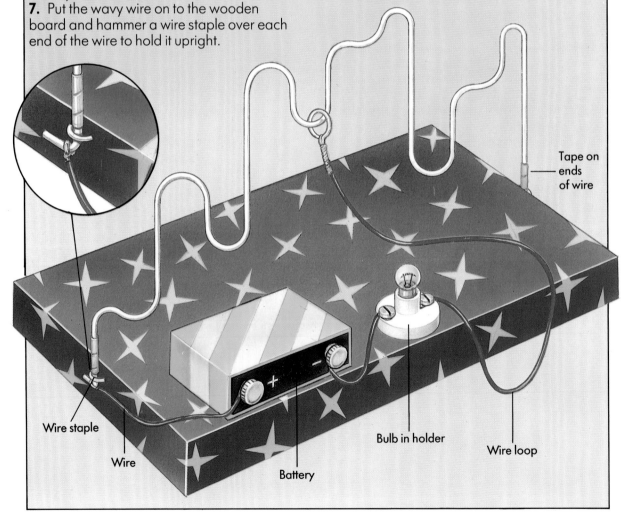

Tape on ends of wire

Wire staple

Wire

Battery

Bulb in holder

Wire loop

Electronic Quiz Game

Make a quiz game with a light that flashes to show the right answer.

1. On one side of the card, glue or tape some pieces of paper with the questions on the left and the answers on the right. Muddle them up so each question is next to the wrong answer.

2. Push a paper fastener through the card next to each question and each answer.

3. Turn the quiz board over and join up each question to the right answer with a piece of wire. Loop the wire around the back of the paper fasteners.

4. With some more wire, join the battery to the bulb holder as shown in the diagram.

5. Join some more wire to the other side of the battery and the other side of the bulb holder. Leave the ends of both these wires free.

Equipment: A piece of stiff card about 30 cm (1 foot) square, paper, pen, scissors, pins, brass paper fasteners, wire, battery, bulb in a bulb holder, sticky tape, glue.

How to play the game

Ask a friend to hold one of the loose wires on a paper fastener next to a question and the other loose wire on a paper fastener next to the answer they think is the right one. If they are correct, they will complete a circuit and the bulb will light up.

More things to try

Make up some different questions and answers for your quiz board but don't forget to connect each question to the correct answer on the back of the board.

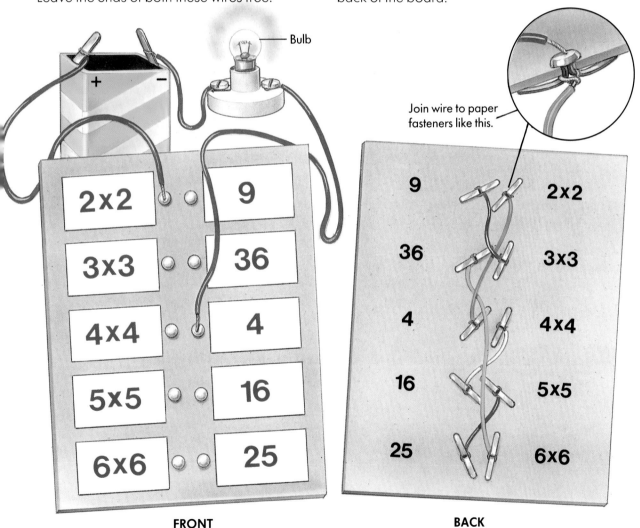

Bulb

Join wire to paper fasteners like this.

FRONT

BACK

Make a Morse Code Transmitter

In 1838, an American, Samuel Morse, invented a way of sending messages by means of electrical signals. He worked out a code of short and long sounds or flashes of light which represented all the letters of the alphabet. The code was named the **Morse Code** after its inventor.

You can send messages from one room to another by making a simple morse code transmitter.

Equipment: Two wires long enough to stretch between the two rooms, two bulbs in bulb holders (or two small buzzers), two batteries, two paper clip switches (*see page 65*).

1. Make two switches but bend the paper clips up in the air above the drawing pins.
2. Connect the batteries and bulbs at the ends of the two long wires to match the diagram.
3. When you touch the drawing pin with the paper clip, you will complete the circuit and both bulbs and buzzers will work. This means you can see the messages you are sending as well as the ones you receive.
4. To send your messages, use the morse code or make up your own secret code.

▲ An operator sends a message on a Morse-printing telegraph.

Morse Code

a	● ━	s	● ● ●
b	━ ● ● ●	t	━
c	━ ● ━ ●	u	● ● ━
d	━ ● ●	v	● ● ● ━
e	●	w	● ━ ━
f	● ● ━ ●	x	━ ● ● ━
g	━ ━ ●	y	━ ● ━ ━
h	● ● ● ●	z	━ ━ ● ●
i	● ●	1	● ━ ━ ━ ━
j	● ━ ━ ━	2	● ● ━ ━ ━
k	━ ● ━	3	● ● ● ━ ━
l	● ━ ● ●	4	● ● ● ● ━
m	━ ━	5	● ● ● ● ●
n	━ ●	6	━ ● ● ● ●
o	━ ━ ━	7	━ ━ ● ● ●
p	● ━ ━ ●	8	━ ━ ━ ● ●
q	━ ━ ● ━	9	━ ━ ━ ━ ●
r	● ━ ●	0	━ ━ ━ ━ ━

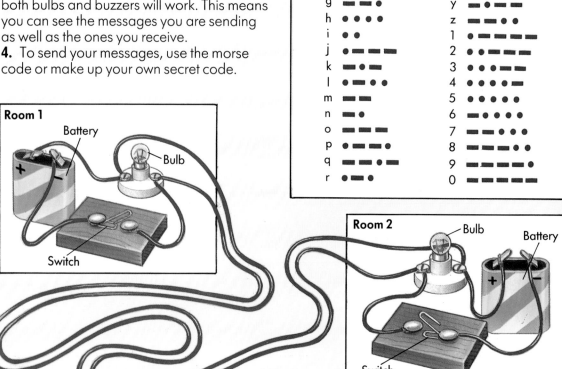

Room 1
Battery
Bulb
Switch

Room 2
Bulb
Battery
Switch

Make your own Torch

Sometimes it is very useful to be able to carry an electric light about with you. With a torch, you can see in the dark anywhere and at any time.

Here's how to make your own torch.

Equipment: An empty washing-up liquid bottle, scissors, tin foil, glue, sticky tape, bulb in a bulb holder, 2 brass paper fasteners, paper clip, wire, 2 batteries.

1. Pull off the cap from the washing-up bottle.
2. Use the scissors to cut off the top of the bottle. Turn it upside down to make a funnel.
3. On the inside of the funnel, glue some tin foil.
4. Push the bulb in its holder up inside the neck of the funnel and hold it in position with tape or glue.
5. To make a switch, push the two paper fasteners through the side of the bottle. Use a paper clip and wires to complete the switch.
6. Tape the two batteries together and tape one of the wires from the switch to the base of the batteries.
7. Join the wire from the other side of the switch to the bulb holder.
8. To complete the circuit, use a third wire to join the bulb holder to the top of the batteries.
9. Then stand the batteries inside the bottle or wedge them in with crumpled-up newspaper.
10. Glue or tape the funnel in position in the top of the bottle.

How it works
When you press down on the switch, you complete the circuit. Electricity flows from the batteries to the bulb, which lights up. The tin foil behind the bulb reflects the light back out of the torch so a wider beam of light shines out of the torch.

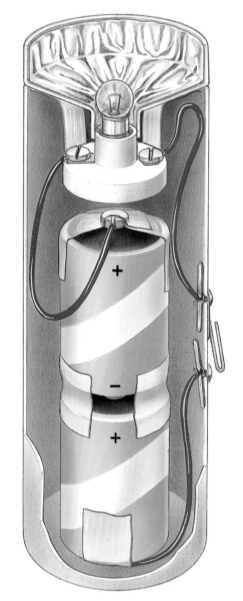

▶ A security worker uses a torch to check the lock on a gate.

Magic Magnets

More than 2000 years ago, the Ancient Greeks discovered a strange rock which could attract pieces of iron. Nearly 1000 years later, Chinese sailors used a piece of the same kind of rock to make a simple compass for their ships. If they hung the rock from a thread, they found that it always pointed North and South.

Nowadays, one name for this rock is **lodestone**, which means 'the stone that leads'. Another name is **magnetite**, which comes from the area of Magnesia, where the rock was first discovered. Materials with the same properties as magnetite can be made into magnets.

Looking at Magnets

Most modern magnets are made from iron or steel. Some are long and straight; they are called bar magnets. Others are shaped like a horseshoe. Small pieces of metal called **keepers** help to stop horseshoe magnets losing their magnetic force when they are not being used.

Magnetic Attraction

All you need is a magnet and a collection of things to test, such as a metal spoon, a glass jar, a plastic pot, keys, tin foil, coins, paper clips, an eraser, nuts and bolts, needles and pins, small stones and a pencil.

Try this experiment to see which materials are attracted to a magnet.
Touch the end of your magnet to each of the objects in your collection. Some of them will seem to stick to the end of the magnet as if they are glued there. Now try moving the magnet slowly towards each object and watch carefully. Small things will seem to leap towards the magnet. Put all the things that stick to the magnet in a separate pile. What are they made from?

More things to try

Does a magnet attract objects along its whole length or just at the ends?

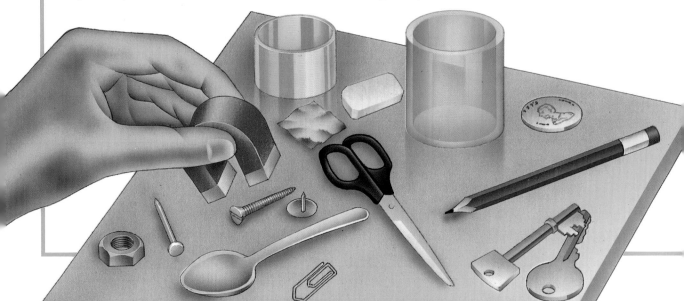

How Strong are Magnets?

If you have several magnets, this experiment will help you to discover which one is the strongest.

Dip the end of one magnet into a box of dressmaker's pins or metal paper clips and, very gently, lift up the magnet. Lots of the pins or paper clips will cling to the magnet. Carefully pull them off and count how many you have picked up.

Now repeat the test with each of the other magnets in turn. Keep a note of the number of pins or paper clips each magnet attracts. The strongest magnet will pick up the highest number of pins or paper clips.

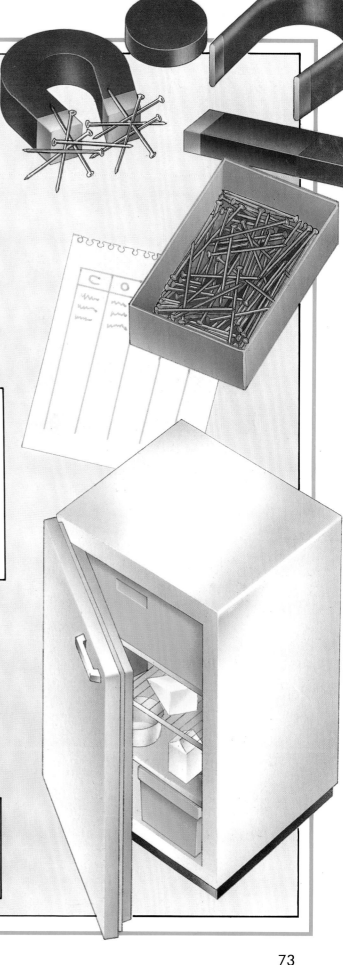

More things to try
- Can you find the strongest part of each magnet?
- Do both ends of a bar magnet have the same magnetic pull?
- Do bigger magnets have a stronger magnetic force than smaller magnets?
- Can you pick up more pins with both ends of a horseshoe magnet or with one end of a bar magnet?

▶ A magnetic catch helps to keep the door of a refrigerator shut. This is a safety device in case a small child climbs inside and shuts the door. If the door had an ordinary catch, the child would not be able to open it from the inside. But with a magnetic catch, the door can be pushed open from the inside.

There are also magnets inside other machines such as televisions, telephones and radios.

Warning
Do not put a magnet near a watch, a clock or a television screen. Magnets could damage these objects.

Stopping the Force

Equipment: A strong magnet, paper, tin foil, a handkerchief, a plastic bag, pins or paper clips.

Do magnetic forces pass through things, in the same way that light passes through a window? Or can the power of a magnet be blocked by putting something in its way or by wrapping something around the magnet? Try this investigation to find out.

Wrap the magnet in the paper and see if it will pick up any pins or paper clips. Then repeat the test with the magnet wrapped in the plastic or the foil or the handkerchief.

How many layers of each material do you need to stop the magnet picking up any pins or paper clips?

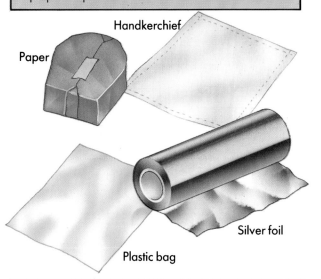

Handkerchief

Paper

Silver foil

Plastic bag

The Magic Butterfly Trick

Equipment: A magnet, a sheet of stiff card, a paper clip, sticky tape, paper, crayons or paints, scissors.

1. Draw a large picture of a butterfly on the paper and colour it in with the crayons or paints.
2. Use the scissors to cut out the butterfly.
3. Stick the paper clip underneath the butterfly.
4. Prop up the sheet of card on some books.
5. Hold the butterfly on one side of the card and hold the magnet right behind it on the other side of the card.
6. As you move the magnet, the butterfly will move over the board as if by magic.

How it works
The force around the magnet attracts the metal paper clip and pulls the butterfly around the board.

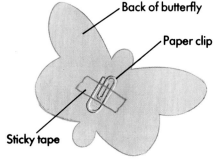

Back of butterfly

Paper clip

Sticky tape

Make a Fishing Game

Equipment: A thin stick or garden cane, a large cardboard box, thin card, crayons or paints, paper clips, cotton or string, sticky tape, scissors, a small magnet.

1. Draw and colour ten fish shapes on the thin card and cut them out.
2. Write a different number on each fish.
3. Stick a paper clip on the back of each fish.
4. Decorate the large box to make it look like a fish tank and put the fishes inside the tank.
5. To make a fishing rod, tape or tie the small magnet to one end of some strong cotton or string. Tie the other end of the cotton or string to the stick or cane.

How to play the game
This game needs two players. Take it in turns to use the magnetic rod to pull a fish out of the box. To keep the score, count up the numbers on the fish you catch.

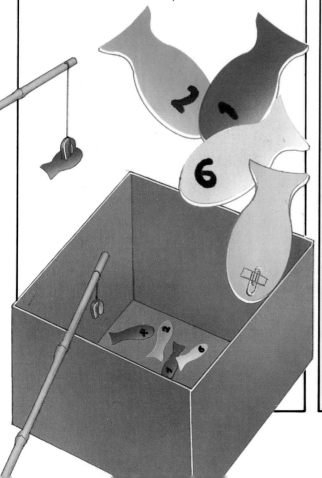

Magnetic Boating Game

Equipment: Magnetic fishing rods (see fishing game), pieces of cork, drawing pins, dressmaker's pins, paper, scissors, crayons or paints, sticky tape or glue, large bowl of water.

1. Make little boats from pieces of cork with a drawing pin pressed into the bottom. To make masts, stick steel pins into the corks.
2. For the sails, draw and colour paper triangles and cut them out. Glue or tape a sail to each mast.
3. Float the boats in the bowl of water.
4. Use the magnetic rods to steer the boats around the bowl and have boat races with your friends.

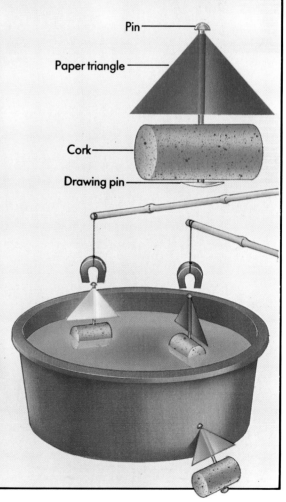

Pin
Paper triangle
Cork
Drawing pin

Test your Driving Skills

1. On the large piece of cardboard, draw and colour a system of roads. Make each road quite wide and include several road junctions, bends and a roundabout.

2. On the thin card, draw and colour a car as if you are looking at it from the side. Make sure the car is small enough to fit on to the roads you have drawn.

3. Cut out the top of the car but leave a flap of card at the bottom. Fold back the flap to make the car stand upright.

4. Push a drawing pin through the flap of card and put a piece of cork or modelling clay on top of the sharp point of the pin.

Equipment: A large piece of stiff cardboard about 30 to 40 cm (12 to 16 inches) square, thin card, crayons or colouring pens, scissors, drawing pins, modelling clay or cork, small magnet, a thin stick or cane, sticky tape, books or bricks.

5. Tape the magnet to the end of the stick or cane.

6. Rest the road system on books or bricks so it is high enough for you to be able to slide the magnet on its stick or cane underneath.

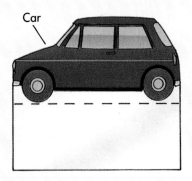

Car

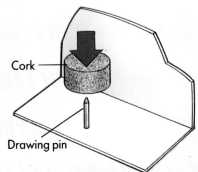

Cork

Drawing pin

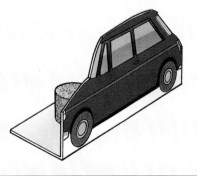

Paper Clip Trick

Put a large glass jar almost full of water on to a table. Drop a paper clip into the jar so it is resting on the side of the jar at the bottom. Can you get the paper clip out of the jar without getting your fingers wet?

If you hold a magnet outside the jar next to the paper clip and slowly slide the magnet up the side of the jar, it will pull the paper clip up with it. When you get to the top of the jar, the paper clip will stick to the magnet and you can lift it out of the jar.

How to play the game

This game needs one or more players. Start with the car in one corner and put the magnet underneath the cardboard directly below the cars. As you move the magnet, you will be able to drive the car along the roads. See how long it takes to drive the car around the course. Add a ten-second penalty every time the car comes off the road.

If your board is large enough and you have two magnets, you could have a race with a friend.

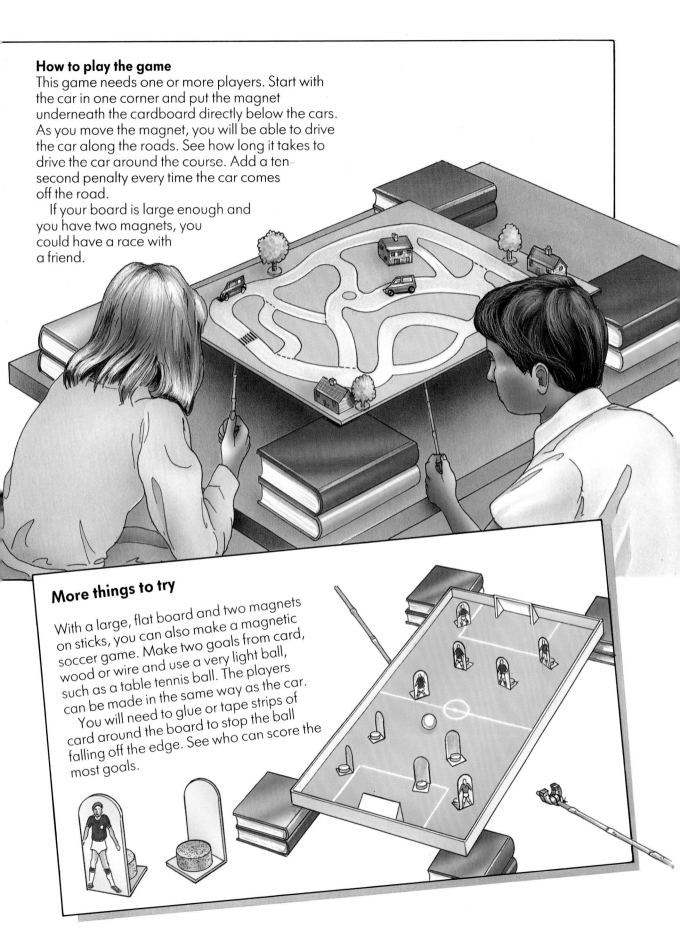

More things to try

With a large, flat board and two magnets on sticks, you can also make a magnetic soccer game. Make two goals from card, wood or wire and use a very light ball, such as a table tennis ball. The players can be made in the same way as the car. You will need to glue or tape strips of card around the board to stop the ball falling off the edge. See who can score the most goals.

Magnetic Forces

The strange invisible force that surrounds a magnet is not fully understood. But if iron filings are sprinkled on to a magnet they show the pattern of this force. The filings cluster together in places where the force is strongest. A lot of filings stick to the ends of the magnet. On the next three pages, you can find out more about these strong forces at the ends of a magnet.

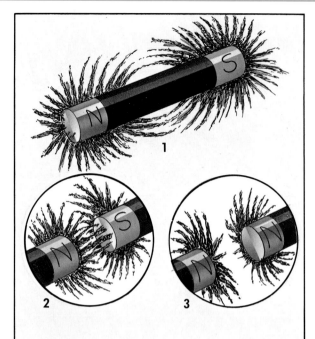

Iron filings show the lines of force around a magnet (**1**). Unlike poles attract each other (**2**); like poles repel each other (**3**).

Pushing and Pulling

The ends of a magnet are called **poles** and every magnet has a North Pole and a South Pole. The North Pole is sometimes red and the South Pole is sometimes blue or plain metal.

Tie a thread around a bar magnet so it balances horizontally when you let it swing freely. The magnet will turn so the North Pole faces North and the South Pole faces South. (You can check the direction with a compass.)

With two strong magnets, you can discover some fascinating facts about the poles of a magnet. Lay one magnet on a smooth surface and slide the other one towards it so a pole of one magnet is close to a pole of the other magnet. The two magnets will either spring together or try to push each other away. You will find that two North Poles or two South Poles will push away (repel) each other but a North Pole and a South Pole will attract each other.

More things to try

Tape a magnet on to the roof of a toy car and tape another magnet on to the roof of a second car. Make sure that the two North Poles or the two South Poles of the magnets are on the front of both cars. If you roll the two cars towards each other, the two like poles will repel each other and push the cars apart.

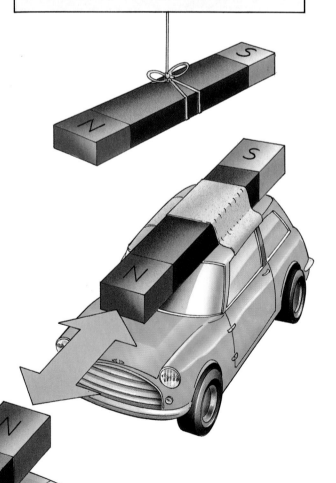

Magnetic Train

The force of strong magnets pushing away from each other is used in some high-speed trains. Both the train and the track contain powerful magnets which work only when electricity flows through them. This means they can be switched on and off.

The magnets are arranged so the North Poles of the track magnets face upwards and the North Poles of the train magnets face downwards. When the magnets are turned on, the two North Poles repel each other. This lifts the train clear of the track so it hovers above the rail. The train can move very easily like this and so it travels much faster than an ordinary train.

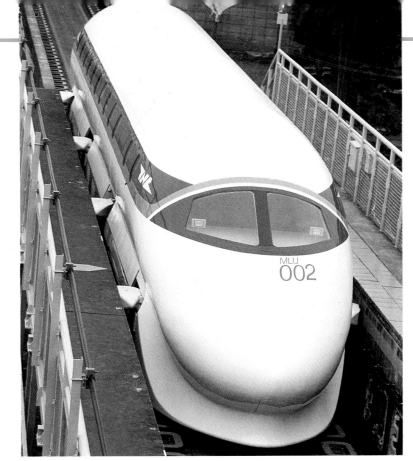

▲ The test run of the new MLU-002 in Japan.

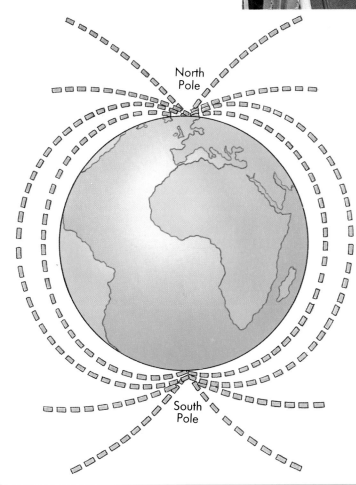

The Magnetic Earth

The Earth acts as if it has a gigantic bar magnet along its centre. Lines of magnetic force run through the Earth from one pole to another. The needle of a compass is a small magnet and it lines up with the Earth's magnetic field so it always points North and South. (The magnet in the experiment on page 78 pointed North and South for the same reason.)

A compass needle does not point to the true North Pole. Instead it points to a spot somewhere in Canada which is a long way to the west of the true North Pole. The Earth's magnetic forces are always changing slightly, so the position of magnetic north changes slightly each year. Hundreds of years from now, magnetic north will be to the east of the North Pole. Magnetic south is also in a different place from the true South Pole.

Make a Compass

Equipment: A large needle, a small piece of cork or polystyrene, a magnet, a saucer of water.

First you need to turn the needle into a magnet; this is called **magnetizing** the needle. To do this, stroke one pole of the magnet gently along the whole length of the needle in the same direction 20 times.

Inside the needle, the little particles (**domains**) which make up the metal are usually pointing in different directions. As you stroke the needle with the magnet, the particles all line up and point in the same direction. As long as the particles stay in line, the needle will act like a magnet.

To make your compass, lay the magnetized needle on a piece of cork or polystyrene and float it in a saucer of water. The needle will swing round to point in a North-South direction, just like a real compass needle.

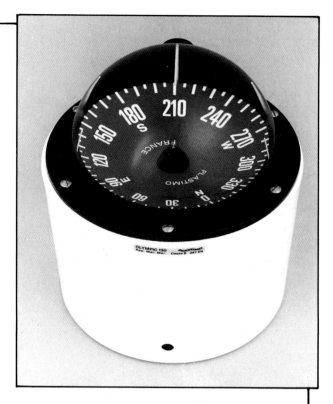

▲ A compass is especially important for navigating at sea. Nautical compasses are designed to stay level no matter how much the boat bobs up and down on the waves.

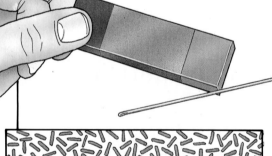

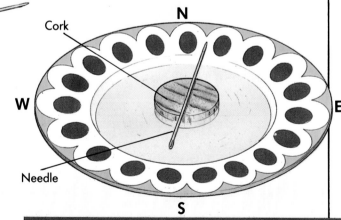

Cork

Needle

Warning
If you drop or bang a magnet you will shake up the particles so they move out of line. The magnet will then lose its magnetic powers.

Making Magnets with Electricity

In about 1820 a Danish scientist, Hans Christian Ørsted, discovered that electricity flowing through a wire close to a compass needle made the needle swing away from the North-South direction.

Scientists have since found many links between electricity and magnetism. For example, when electricity flows through a coil of wire which is wrapped around an iron or steel bar, the bar turns into a magnet. It is called an **electro-magnet**.

Make an Electro-magnet

Equipment: A battery, a switch (*see page 65*), an iron or steel nail about 15 cm (6 inches) long, some covered wire about 60 to 100 cm (2 to 3 feet) long, a box of pins or paper clips.

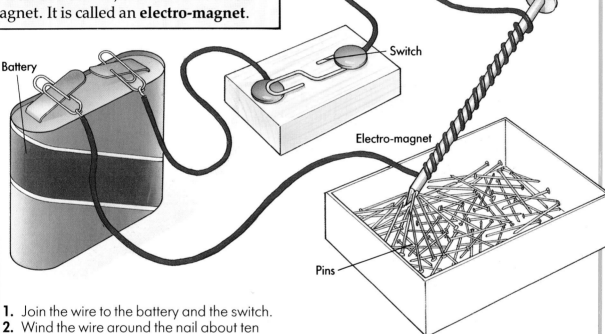

Battery

Switch

Nail

Electro-magnet

Pins

1. Join the wire to the battery and the switch.
2. Wind the wire around the nail about ten times.
3. Join the other end of the wire to the battery terminal to complete the circuit.
4. Switch on the electric current and dip the end of the nail into the box of pins or paper clips. What happens? Are any pins or clips attracted to your electro-magnet?
5. Switch off the current. What happens now?
6. Now wind the wire around the nail ten more times and repeat the experiment. Can you pick up any pins this time?
7. Finally, wind the wire in tight coils along most of the nail. (You may need to use some sticky tape to hold the wire in place.)
8. Repeat the experiment to see if the extra wire makes the magnet weaker or stronger.

How it works
The electricity flowing through the tight coils of wire creates a strong magnetic force from one end of the coil to the other. The force lines up all the magnetic particles in the nail and turns it into a magnet. With more wire coils, the magnetic force is stronger.

If your nail is made from iron, you will find that when you switch off the electricity, the pins or clips fall off the nail. Iron is only magnetic as long as electricity is flowing in the wire. It is a **temporary** magnet. But if your nail is made from steel, it stays magnetic even when the electricity is switched off. It is a **permanent** magnet.

Make an Electro-magnetic Crane

This crane will lift small steel objects when you switch on the electricity.

1. Make a hole in the top of both the square boxes.

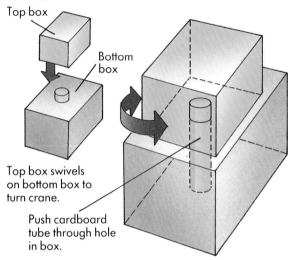

Top box

Bottom box

Top box swivels on bottom box to turn crane.

Push cardboard tube through hole in box.

Equipment: An electro-magnet with an iron nail (*see page 81*), small cardboard boxes (two square ones and one long, thin one), a cardboard tube, two cotton reels, some strong thread, glue, sticky tape, scissors, paper clips or pins.

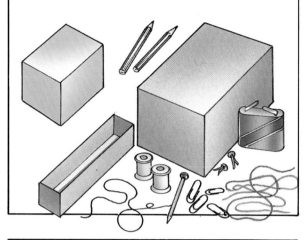

2. Push the cardboard tube down into one box and fit the other box on top of the tube.
3. Cut off both ends of the long, thin box.
4. Tie the thread to one cotton reel. Fix this reel in one end of the long, thin box by pushing a pencil through the side of the box and right through the middle of the reel.
5. Use another pencil to fix the other cotton reel in the other end of the long box and hang the thread over the top of the reel. Leave the thread hanging out of the box.

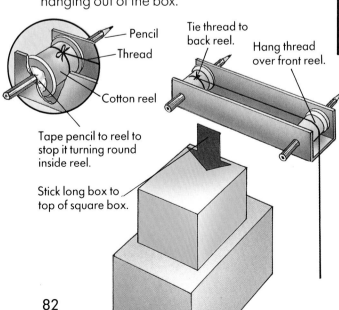

Pencil

Thread

Cotton reel

Tape pencil to reel to stop it turning round inside reel.

Stick long box to top of square box.

Tie thread to back reel.

Hang thread over front reel.

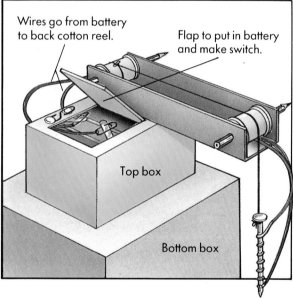

Wires go from battery to back cotton reel.

Flap to put in battery and make switch.

Top box

Bottom box

6. Glue or tape the long, thin box on top of the square box.
7. Put the battery inside the top square box and join it to a switch on the top of this box. Join the battery and the switch to the nail with some more wire, as shown in the diagram.
8. Lay the wires under the cotton reels and tie the nail to the end of the thread.
9. Decorate the outside of the crane with paints or crayons.

▶ Very large electro-magnets with iron cores are used to sort scrap metal. They attract all the iron and steel and separate them from the other metals.

10. Turn the crane so the nail is above the paper clips or pins. To lower the nail, turn the pencil on the back cotton reel.
11. To turn the nail into an electro-magnet, switch on the electricity. See how many pins are attracted to the nail.

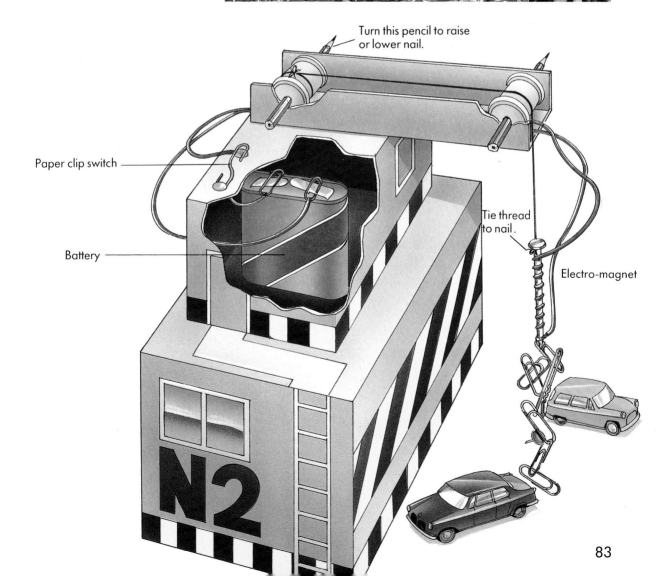

Turn this pencil to raise or lower nail.

Paper clip switch

Battery

Tie thread to nail.

Electro-magnet

N2

Animals and Electricity

Most animals use electrical signals (**nerve impulses**) to send messages to different parts of the body. In humans, these messages travel through a network of nerve cells which link the organs of sight, hearing, smell, taste and touch to the brain. The brain is constantly sending and receiving electrical messages as it reacts to information about conditions inside and outside the body. The amount of electricity in our bodies is very, very tiny, but some animals, such as electric fishes, can generate massive amounts of electricity.

Electric Fishes

An electric eel (*above*) uses modified muscle cells along the sides of its body to generate electricity and respond to electrical signals. It can produce sudden, massive electric shocks of 500 volts, which could kill a horse or stun a person. It uses this electric power to capture and kill food or drive away attackers. Electric eels also produce low-voltage electrical signals which help them to find their way around and communicate with other fishes.

Passing on messages

At the point where one nerve cell meets another, there is a tiny gap called a **synapse**. When a nerve impulse reaches a synapse, it is changed from an electrical message into a chemical message. This can 'jump across' the gap and trigger an electrical nerve impulse in the next nerve cell.

Nerve impulses can travel at very high speeds. Some of the nerves inside our bodies can send impulses at 150 metres (490 feet) per second.

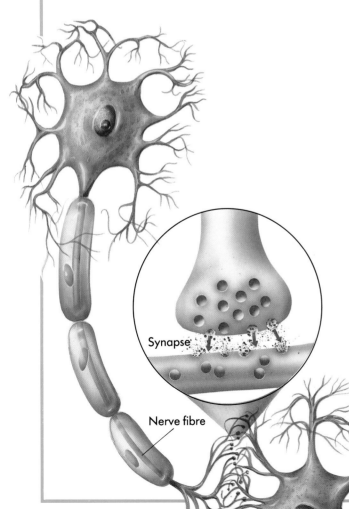

Synapse

Nerve fibre

Using Electricity

Electricity has changed our lives at home, at school and at work. Electric motors drive all sorts of machines, from vacuum cleaners to electric drills, which help us to do jobs more quickly and easily. We use electricity to keep warm in winter and cool in summer, and to provide light all the year round. Electricity works fans and air conditioning systems as well as refrigerators and freezers. Electricity makes pictures appear on television and computer screens. It can make clocks work and be used to switch machines on and off at set times. How do you think electricity might be used to help us in the future?

In the Hospital

In hospital, electricity powers X-ray machines, kidney machines (*see photograph below*), incubators for premature babies and all sorts of other vital equipment which helps people to recover from accidents or illnesses.

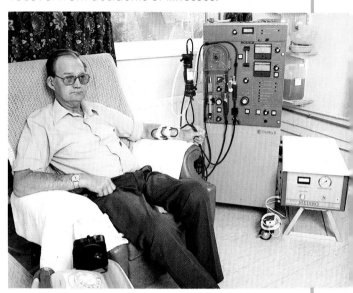

On the Farm

Farmers make use of many electrical machines, such as this milking machine. Machines help the farmer to give farm animals the right amount of feed. Young chicks can be reared under the warmth of electric heaters. Electric fans can be used to dry grain and keep it fresh, and electric conveyor belts make it easier to move straw and grain. Farming machines save time and do much of the heavy work.

In the Greenhouse

Automatic electric controls ensure that greenhouse crops are given ideal growing conditions all the year round, no matter what the weather is like outside. Electric thermostats control heating and ventilation, and electric irrigation systems make sure the right amount of moisture reaches the plants.

Electricity for Transport

Electricity is a cheap form of power for some cars and trucks. These vehicles carry their electrical power in batteries which are large and very heavy; the batteries also have to be re-charged at frequent intervals when their electricity is used up. At the moment, there are no batteries which are small enough, light enough and powerful enough to make a car go fast for hundreds of miles. But one may be developed in the future. The advantages of electrically-powered vehicles are that they are quieter than vehicles with petrol or diesel engines and they do not pollute the atmosphere.

In the Factory

In factories, electrical machines such as fork-lift trucks (*above*) are used to move heavy objects from place to place. Tools such as electric drills, saws and paint sprayers also save a lot of time and heavy work.

Electricity drives the robots (*left*) which assemble products such as cars and computers faster and more accurately than people can. It also provides the heating for ovens and furnaces which melt metals or bake clay into bricks.

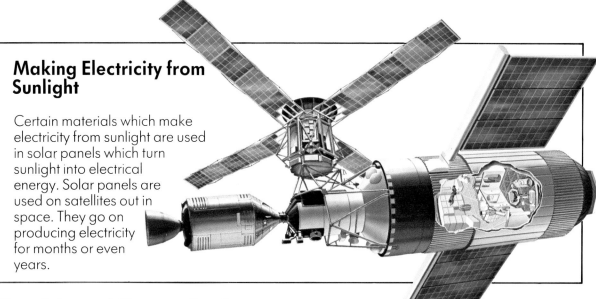

Making Electricity from Sunlight

Certain materials which make electricity from sunlight are used in solar panels which turn sunlight into electrical energy. Solar panels are used on satellites out in space. They go on producing electricity for months or even years.

Electricity and Communications

Electricity is vital for communication systems. Radios and television sets receive electro-magnetic signals transmitted from broadcasting stations. Telephones turn the sound of our voices into electrical signals which travel along the network of wires connecting telephones together.

The miniature electrical circuits in microchips have revolutionized the development of calculators and computers. A microchip contains thousands of electrical components on a piece of silicon smaller than a pin-head.

▲ In this picture of Chicago, you can see some of the street lights, car headlamps and light bulbs which light up the city at night. What would the picture look like if there was a power cut? Can you imagine living with only candles and fire to provide light, warmth and power?

◄ A wafer of silicon containing hundreds of microchips.

Electricity and Magnets Quiz

1. Magnets attract every kind of metal.

2. These bulbs are joined in parallel. If one bulb is removed, will the others stay alight?

True or False?

3. Electricity moves through circuits in the same direction.

True or False?

4. The nerves in your body transmit messages using electricity.

5. What is wrong with these pictures?

Spot the Mistakes

Answers

1. *False. Magnets mainly attract metals containing iron (page 72).*

2. *True. If a bulb is removed, the other two will still have circuits back to the battery. If the bulbs were joined in series, removing one bulb would make the others go out (page 63).*

3. *True. Direct current electricity always travels in the same direction (page 62).*

4. *True. Nerves transmit all messages around the body and to and from the brain as electrical impulses (page 84).*

5. *Top left: The bulb will not light when the batteries are connected by their negative terminals. They must be connected positive to negative (page 62). Bottom left: Similar poles of two magnets will always repel each other (page 78). Right: Lightning will always strike the highest point on the ground, such as this church tower. Tall buildings use lightning conductors to lead the charge harmlessly to the ground (page 57).*

SIMPLE CHEMISTRY

This section of the book will help you to investigate simple chemistry.
Think about chemistry when you are in the kitchen, when you mix things
or when you touch, smell or taste almost anything.

There are eight main topics in this section:

- How chemicals make up the world
- Atoms and molecules
- How chemicals react together
- Coloured chemicals
- Chemicals as solids, liquids and gases
- Chemicals that are metals
- Chemicals containing carbon
- Chemical factories, waste and pollution

**Use the symbols below to help you
identify the three kinds of practical
activities in this book.**

EXPERIMENTS

TRICKS

THINGS TO MAKE

Introduction

Everything in the world is made of chemicals. Rocks, soil, houses, bridges, cars, plants and animals—and you. Everything is made from a set of basic chemical substances. Chemistry is the scientific study of how these chemicals are joined to form the objects around us, and how we can split or combine chemicals into new substances.

The questions on these two pages are based on scientific ideas explained in this section. As you carry out the experiments, you can answer these questions, and understand more about how chemicals make up our world.

Safety and equipment

The activities in this section use only common household substances and pieces of equipment. Keep chemicals safe in containers. Wash your hands before and afterwards. Never put chemicals near your face or mess about with them 'to see what happens'. This is neither safe, nor good science.

▲ What is an acid, and how is it different from a base? (pages 104–105)

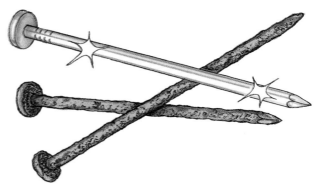

▲ What is a chemical, and what makes it change into another chemical? (pages 92–93)

▼What makes a chemical change from a solid, to liquid, to gas? (pages 108–111)

Pressure of skate blades on ice melts it into water.

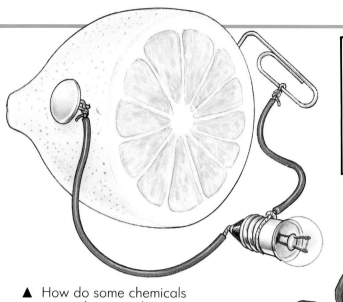

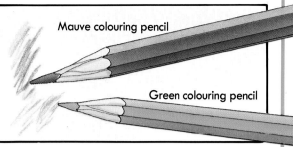

▲ What kinds of properties do chemicals have? (pages 94–95)

▲ How do some chemicals react together to make electricity? (pages 116–117)

▲ What are chemicals themselves made of? (pages 96–97)

▲ How can we all help to save chemicals, and re-use them as much as possible? (page 127)

▼ What makes a metal a metal? (pages 114–115)

▲ How can different chemicals be separated from a mixture? (pages 98–101)

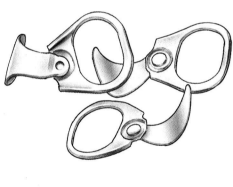

▼ What chemical changes go on inside living things? (page 111)

▶ Which chemicals are you made of? (pages 121–123)

Chemical World

'Chemicals' are not just the strangely coloured bubbling liquids in the test-tubes of the scientist's laboratory. Chemicals are all around us, forming everything we smell, taste, touch and see—and even things we cannot see, such as air or glass. Chemistry is happening all the time. Chemicals are changing all the time.

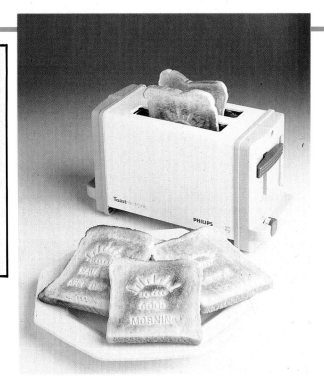

Cooking Chemicals

The kitchen is one of the best places to see chemistry in action. We eat certain foods raw, but others must be cooked in some way. Cooking makes them safe to eat, or improves their taste, or makes them easily digested by the body. Cooking changes the chemicals in foods, usually by heat. As a piece of bread is heated in a toaster, its surface burns and becomes crispy, and its colour changes to brown. A raw egg has a runny, slippery 'white' and a thick, yellow liquid yolk. Boil it in water and both these substances turn solid, to produce a hard-boiled egg. Or heat a raw

▲ Toast is simply bread which has been 'lightly burned' on each side. Burning usually changes chemicals in a drastic way (page 97).

egg in a pan and stir it with butter and milk, and it changes to scrambled egg, which is light yellow and lumpy.

Browned toast made from white bread.

Hard-boiled egg

Scrambled egg

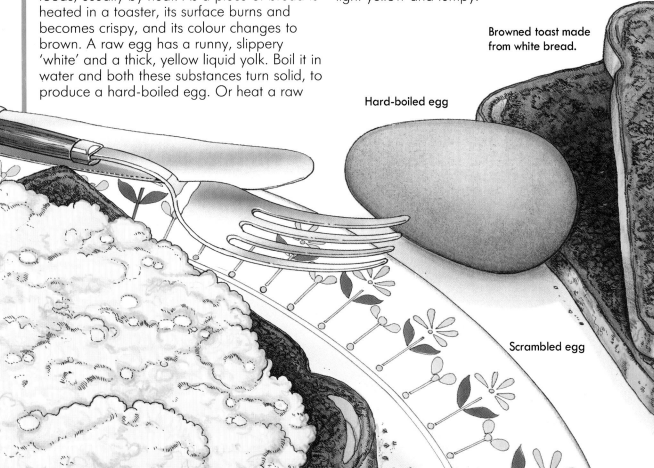

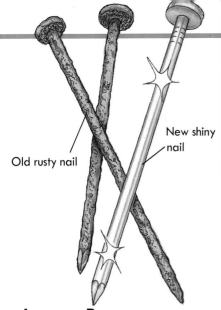

Old rusty nail

New shiny nail

Iron to Rust

▶▲ Iron, a metal (*page 114*), goes rusty if it becomes damp. The iron combines with water to make a new substance, reddy-brown rust. Leave a new iron nail in a dry place, such as an airing cupboard. Put other nails in a damp place, like a corner of the garden. Which ones go rusty? Old cars, beds and many other objects have iron in them, and rust too.

Going Hot While Setting

Fresh plaster of Paris is soft and powdery. Mix it with water, leave it, and it becomes very hard. But the plaster does not 'dry', in the way a towel dries on the clothes line. It goes through a chemical change when mixed with water, 'sets' to produce a new substance, and produces heat. Mix some plaster with water in a plastic container. After 30 minutes, the side of the container should feel warm. **Caution:** Do not throw leftover plaster into the sink. It sets even under water!

Equipment: Plaster of Paris, plastic container.

Margarine container

Setting plaster of Paris

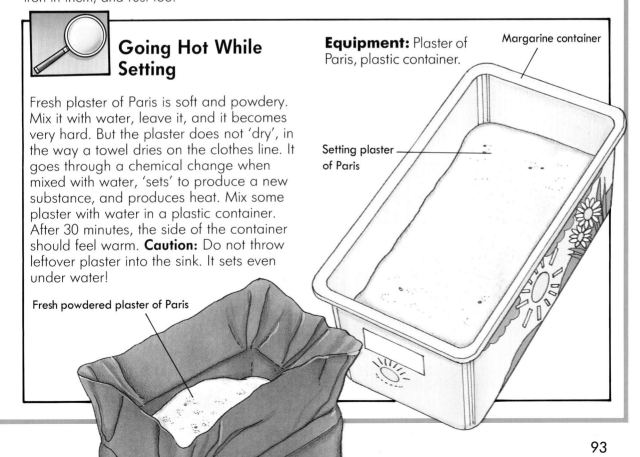

Fresh powdered plaster of Paris

Chemical Properties

How can we identify a chemical? We can use our senses to detect its properties. We look at colour and shininess. Provided a chemical is safe we can smell its odour, feel its hardness and texture and weight, and taste its flavour.

The basic properties of any chemical are always the same, no matter what the shapes of the objects made from it. Aluminium is a metal used to make 'tin foil'. It is also used, as much thicker sheets, to make the bodies and wings of aircraft.

▶ Floppy cooking foil seems to be made of a very different material from an aircraft. Yet they are both aluminium.

Testing Properties

Lemon   Potato

Chemicals may look and feel the same, but taste quite different. Ask a friend to grind up small amounts of sugar, salt and chalk. Place them in separate piles on a plate. Which is which? Taste is the best way to tell them apart. **Caution:** Never taste an unknown substance. It could be poisonous.

There are two small pools of yellowish liquid chemicals on a plate. One is lemon juice, the other is cooking oil. How can you tell them apart? The easiest way is by touch. Rub them between your fingers. The cooking oil feels thick and slippery, and the lemon juice is thin and watery.

Taste

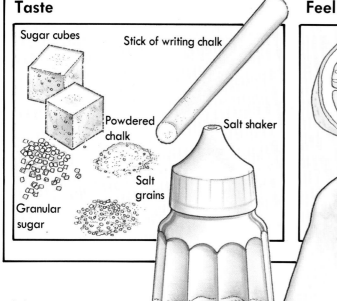

Sugar cubes

Stick of writing chalk

Powdered chalk

Salt shaker

Salt grains

Granular sugar

Feel

Fresh lemon

Cooking oil

Colour

You could not colour a picture with your eyes closed. Even if you knew where to draw you would not be able to choose the correct colour of pencil without looking. Different coloured pencils feel and smell the same. They can only be told apart by sight. You might end up with a very strange-looking picture indeed! Colour is an important property of chemicals, because eyesight is an important sense for us.

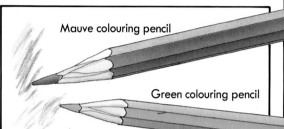

Mauve colouring pencil

Green colouring pencil

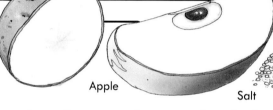

Apple

Salt

Sugar   Polystyrene

Chalk

A smell consists of tiny particles of odour chemicals floating in the air. As you sniff, the chemicals are detected by special nerves inside your nose. Substances which look and feel similar can sometimes be distinguished by smell. Cut small lumps of apple and potato. Give each a sniff to tell them apart.

Some chemicals are very heavy for their size, like the metal lead. Others are extremely light. Paint a pebble-shaped lump of expanded polystyrene to look like a stone, and place it next to a real stone. Ask a friend to lift each one. The friend will probably be surprised at the lightness of one of the 'pebbles'!

Smell

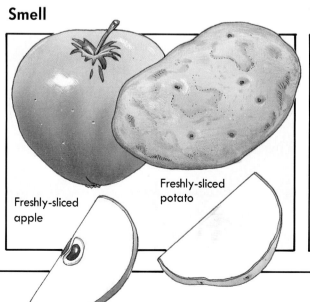

Freshly-sliced potato

Freshly-sliced apple

Weight

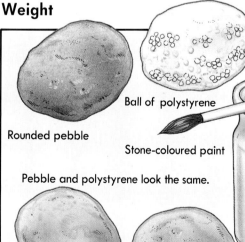

Ball of polystyrene

Rounded pebble

Stone-coloured paint

Pebble and polystyrene look the same.

Building Blocks

There are about 200 basic chemicals, called **elements**. Each element is made of building blocks called **atoms**. These are too small to see even under a microscope. All the atoms of an element are the same as each other, and they are different from the atoms of any other element. Atoms can be split into smaller particles, but these do not have the properties of the element.

Atoms, Molecules and Elements

An element is a pure, single chemical. Iron is an example of an element. No matter how many times a piece of iron is divided, it still has the properties of iron—until, if you could carry on dividing for long enough, you are left with just one atom of iron. An atom is the smallest particle of the element that still has that element's properties. Atoms are rarely found on their own. Usually they are joined to other atoms, to form **molecules**. A molecule may be made of two atoms, or three, or many thousands. The atoms in it may all be of the same element, or from a few elements, or from dozens of different elements.

▼ One of the rarest elements on Earth is plutonium 238. It is used as a source of energy in space probes.

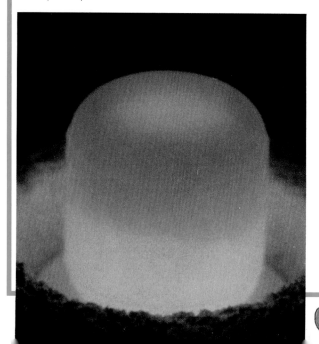

Making Atoms and Molecules

You can make some simple models of atoms, and combine them to give different types of molecules. Two of the commonest elements on Earth are carbon and oxygen. In chemistry, each element has a chemical symbol. The symbol for **carbon** is **C**, and for **oxygen** it is **O**. Just as atoms combine to form molecules, so their symbols can be joined to make a symbol for a molecule. For example, oxygen is in the air we breathe. But it does not occur as single atoms of oxygen, floating around. It exists as molecules of oxygen. Each molecule is made from two oxygen atoms joined together. The simple two-atom molecule of oxygen is written O_2.

Making Playing-Dough Atoms

'Atoms' of different coloured balls of playing-dough can be linked by small sticks, to make different molecules. First, mix two cups of flour and one cup of salt in a saucepan. Add a few drops of food colouring to one cup of water, and stir this thoroughly into the mixture. Also stir in four teaspoons of cream of tartar and two tablespoons of cooking oil. Ask a grown-up to help you warm the pan gently over a low heat, stirring all the time. After the dough thickens, leave it to cool. Make two batches of dough: red for oxygen atoms, and black for carbon atoms.

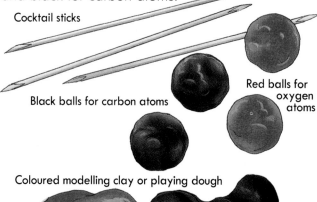

Cocktail sticks

Black balls for carbon atoms

Red balls for oxygen atoms

Coloured modelling clay or playing dough

Equipment: Flour, salt, saucepan, food colouring, cream of tartar, cooking oil.

Carbon

There are several forms of the element carbon, depending on how the carbon atoms are joined together. One familiar form is soot. Wood, coal, heating oil and similar substances contain lots of carbon (*page 118*).

Forms of carbon are graphite (the 'lead' in a pencil) and diamond.

Carbon C

Oxygen

Pure oxygen is made by plants, during the process of photosynthesis. The plant's leaves capture the Sun's light energy and use it to make the plant's food. As this happens, molecules of oxygen are given off into the air.

Most living things need to breathe oxygen in order to stay alive.

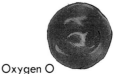

Oxygen O

Carbon Dioxide

Carbon dioxide is a waste product of our body chemistry. As we breathe out, it is released into the air. The harder our muscles work, the more carbon dioxide they make, and so we need to breathe air harder to get rid of it.

Carbon dioxide (CO_2) has one carbon atom and two oxygen atoms.

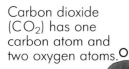

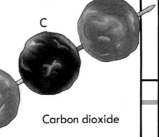

Carbon dioxide

Carbon Monoxide

A car engine combines carbon and oxygen to make carbon monoxide, a poisonous substance in exhaust fumes. Atoms can join only in certain ways, depending on how many links, or 'bonds', they attach to each other.

Carbon monoxide (CO) has one carbon atom and one oxygen atom.

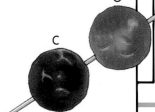

Carbon monoxide

Mixing, Dissolving

Some chemicals can mix together without changing. Stir together powdered chalk and powdered iron (iron filings), and you would not notice any alteration. But other chemicals may react to produce a new kind of chemical (*page 102*). Or one chemical may dissolve in the other.

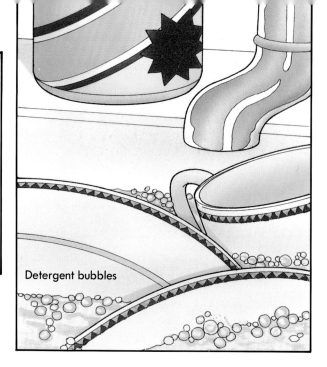

Detergent bubbles

Washing Up With Soap

In dissolving, a solid chemical 'disappears' into a liquid one. We see this every day, when someone puts sugar in tea or coffee, or puts salt in water before cooking. The solid chemical (sugar or salt) is called the solute. The liquid one (tea or water) is the solvent. The two together are known as the solution. The solute alters its nature as it dissolves and 'disappears' in the solution.

How it works: This is because the chemical changes from large groups of solute molecules into very small groups or even single molecules. The solute does not combine chemically with the solvent (*page 100*).

▼ Whether it is a dirty dish or a dirty car, soapy water helps to break up and dissolve the dirt and grime, and wash it away.

Which Chemicals Will Dissolve?

Water is the 'Universal Solvent'. Many substances dissolve in it, to make drinks, inks, cleaning fluids and other useful solutions. You can test whether a substance dissolves by adding a small amount of it to a beaker of clean water, and stirring slowly. If the substance is soluble it will disappear and leave the water clear, though it may give its colour to the water. Tea, coffee, salt and honey should dissolve. Chemicals like sand and cooking oil do not dissolve.

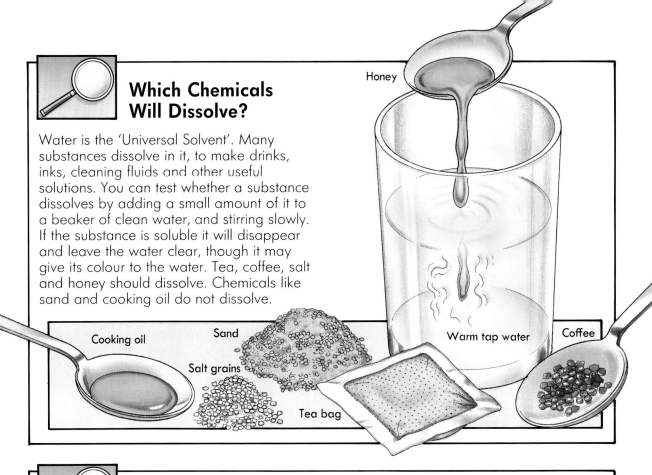

Honey

Warm tap water

Coffee

Cooking oil

Sand

Salt grains

Tea bag

Which Dissolves Best—Hot or Cold Water?

This simple experiment shows that warm water is a better solvent than cold water. You need two identical beakers. Into one, put cool water straight from the cold tap. Put very warm water from the hot tap into the other beaker. Then, add a teaspoon of salt to each beaker, and stir. The salt should dissolve and disappear into the warm water first. What happens if you keep adding salt to each beaker?

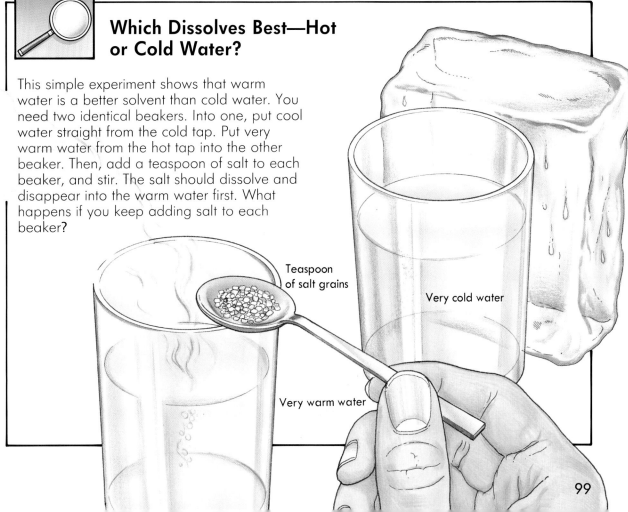

Teaspoon of salt grains

Very cold water

Very warm water

'Un-Dissolving'

When one chemical mixes or dissolves in another, the molecules of each chemical remain basically unchanged. It is possible to separate them again fairly easily. After separation, the chemicals are the same as they were at the beginning. When chemicals react together (*page 102*), separation is more complicated—and may be impossible.

Separating by Evaporation

A solute can be separated or 'un-dissolved' from its solvent by evaporation. In this process, the solution is heated. The solvent gradually turns into a vapour or gas (*page 108*), leaving behind the solute. The vapourized solvent is changed from a gas back into a liquid by cooling so that it condenses. (**Condensation** is the opposite of evaporation.) Ask a grown-up to make a mug of steaming-hot coffee—a solution of coffee chemicals in water. Over the mug, hold a cold saucepan from the fridge. Water vapour condenses on the pan and turns to clear liquid water.

▼ Common salt is used for many purposes, from industrial processes to cooking. Sea water contains dissolved salt. This can be obtained by using the Sun's heat to evaporate sea water in shallow pools, called pans. The water slowly turns into a gas, to leave crystals of salt. The process is known as desalination.

Cold saucepan from fridge

Clear water collects

Mug of hot coffee

Lid of coffee jar

Separating Three Chemicals

How could you sort out a mixture of three chemicals: sand, salt and iron filings (powdered iron)? The answer is to use the chemical properties of each substance. Salt dissolves in water, but the other two do not. So add water to the

1 Dissolve the salt in water and evaporate this to obtain salt crystals.

2 Rub a magnet gently in the mixture to pick up the iron filings.

Equipment:
Salt, sand, iron fillings, magnet, dish.

3 Only sand is left in the dish at the end of the experiment.

mixture, and the salt dissolves to form a solution. Pour this off carefully and leave it in a warm place. The water evaporates, to leave the salt on its own. Next, you need to remove the iron particles from the sand. Iron is magnetic, unlike sand. So gently push a magnet through the mixture and the iron filings stick to it. Tap them off into a another container, to leave only the sand.

Separating Colours

Many coloured inks in felt-tip pens are mixtures of a basic set of coloured dyes (*page 106*), in different amounts. Find out which dyes are in your pens by this simple experiment. (Use a pen with ordinary water-soluble ink, not the special alcohol-soluble kind.) Make a thick blob of ink on a piece of blotting paper. Prop this against some books so that the bottom of the blotting paper is in a jamjar of water, with the blob just above the surface. Water seeps up the paper and carries with it the different dyes, but at different speeds. The rainbow pattern reveals the coloured dyes in your ink.

Equipment:
Ink, blotting paper, jamjar.

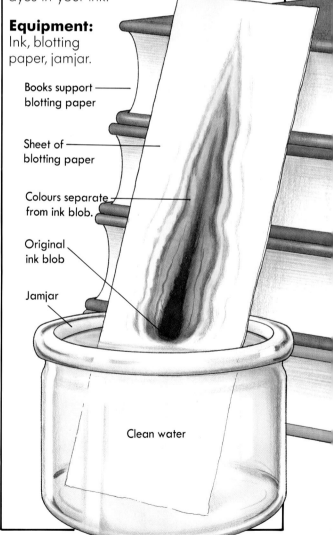

Books support blotting paper

Sheet of blotting paper

Colours separate from ink blob.

Original ink blob

Jamjar

Clean water

101

Chemical Reactions

In a chemical reaction, substances that are mixed together react or combine in some way. They form a new substance, which is different from the original chemicals used to make it. Chemical reactions are going on all around us, as we drive a car, build a wall, cook a meal or paint a door.

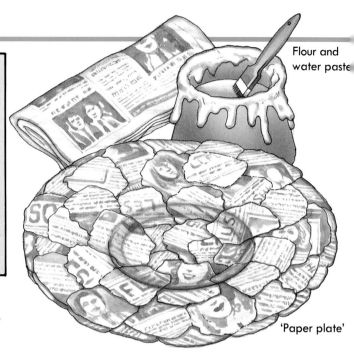

Flour and water paste

'Paper plate'

Equipment: Flour, water, newspaper, plate, petroleum jelly.

Flour-and-Water Paste

Add two cups of flour to one cup of water, and stir to a stiff paste. They become a new substance which is sticky and gooey. This is a chemical reaction involving molecules of starch (*page 122*), one of the main chemicals in flour.

Flour-and-water paste sets hard. Paint layers of old newspaper with it and smooth them onto a mould, such as a plate. (Coat the plate with a thin smear of petroleum jelly, so the paper does not stick to it.) When hard, the plate can be painted in bright colours.

Playing-Dough Sculptures

A simple recipe for playing-dough is given on page 96. In fact, this is a recipe for a chemical reaction. The various ingredients, such as flour and salt, combine to make a new substance, the dough, which has quite different properties. The gentle heat needed to make the dough helps the chemicals to react together. In general, heat speeds up a chemical reaction, while cold slow it down. This is why we put foods in the fridge or freezer to preserve them, by preventing any chemical reactions. It is also why we heat foods in the oven, to make them undergo chemical reactions—what we call 'cooking'.

Playing-dough can be moulded into many shapes, from model people to cups, cars and volcanoes (*see opposite*). If you add some food colouring to the water before you make it, this will give an even colour to the dough. Or you can put the finished models in a gently warm oven to dry them hard.

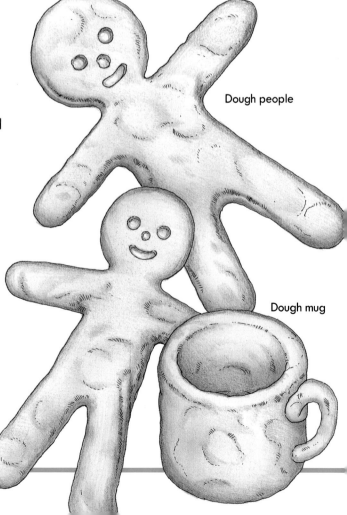

Dough people

Dough mug

Fast and Slow Reactions

▲ A slow reaction, like the setting of cement (*top left*), takes several days. A fast reaction, such as petrol vapour exploding in a car engine (*above*), happens in a fraction of a second.

It is often important to control the rate, or speed, of a chemical reaction. For example, setting cement undergoes a chemical reaction, like plaster-of-Paris (*page 93*) Imagine if cement set a few seconds after being mixed with water! Extra chemicals, 'retardants', can be added to the cement so that it stays soft for longer. A fairly fast chemical reaction happens when baking powder is added to vinegar. You can make a model volcano using this reaction. Mould the sides of the volcano from playing-dough. Put a small pile of baking powder in the hole in the middle, with a few drops of some red food colouring. Then drip in vinegar. Foaming red 'lava' pours from the volcano!

Equipment: Baking powder, vinegar, playing-dough, food colouring.

Vinegar

Baking powder

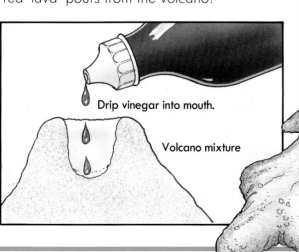

Drip vinegar into mouth.

Volcano mixture

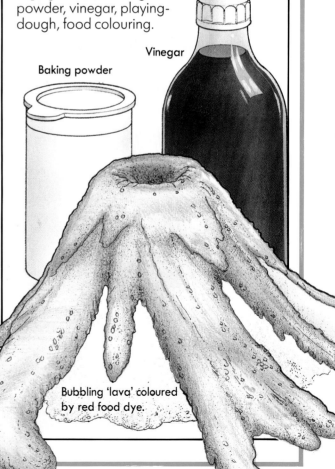

Bubbling 'lava' coloured by red food dye.

Acids and Bases

Chemicals have properties that we can detect, such as colour and smell. Some also have another, more 'chemical' property: they are either acids or bases. These chemicals are important. They react to produce a third group of chemicals, the salts. Acids, bases and salts, and the reactions between them, are used in hundreds of household and industrial processes.

Testing for Acids

Acids are usually sour-tasting and corrosive, which means they 'eat away' other substances. Even a weak acid, like vinegar or lemon juice, has a strongly sour taste. Powerful acids are so corrosive that they should never be touched, let alone tasted. If they splash on you, they will cause stinging pain and eat away your flesh! Acids change the colour of certain chemicals, known as indicators. Bases (see opposite) turn the indicator a different colour.

Equipment: Red cabbage, sieve, pot, bicarbonate of soda, lemon juice.

Red cabbage 'indicator'

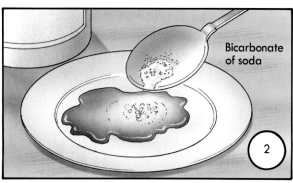

Bicarbonate of soda

Lemon juice

You can make a simple indicator at home, using red cabbage, and test it on some weak acids and bases. Ask a grown-up to chop up about half a red cabbage, bring it to the boil in water, stir well and leave it to soak for about 15 minutes. Pour the water through a sieve. This purple-blue water is your indicator (1). If you add a base to it, like bicarbonate of soda (see opposite), it should turn pale or greeny-blue (2). If you add an acid, like lemon juice, it should turn reddish or pink (3).

Make Mine Green and Fizzy!

A **base** is the 'opposite' of an acid. It tastes bitter, rather than sour, and has a slimy feel. Powerful bases, such as drain-cleaning fluid, are as dangerous as acids and can corrode your skin. However, not all bases are this strong. A weak base is bicarbonate of soda, used in cooking, which can make gingerbread rise.

Equipment: Food colouring, jug, icing sugar, bicarbonate of soda, lemon juice.

How it works:

Add a few drops of green food colouring to a jug of water. Stir in two tablespoons of icing sugar and three teaspoons of bicarbonate of soda. Then add six teaspoons of fresh lemon juice. The acid lemon juice and bicarbonate base react to make carbon dioxide.

Home-made fizzy drink

Lemon juice

Food dye

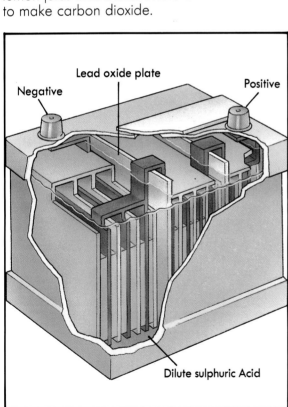

Negative

Lead oxide plate

Positive

Dilute sulphuric Acid

Indigestion tablets

Tea leaves

Coffee beans

▲ A car battery contains very strong sulphuric acid. Goggles should be worn when working with such batteries.

▲ Some medicines are weak bases. The substances obtained from plants, like tea and coffee, are bases called alkaloids.

Colour Chemistry

Not all creatures can see in colour. Humans can. Colours are very important to us, from the beauty of a fine work of art to the red warning light on a control panel. Colour is a property of many chemicals. Some chemicals have especially strong or bright colours. We call these pigments dyes and colourings. They are used to give colour to other objects, from a shirt to a ceiling!

▶ Materials such as wool and cotton can have their own natural colours. But we can change these by dyeing. Coloured chemicals are used to stain the material.

Mixing Colours

This book would not look so bright and interesting if it was printed with just black ink, in 'black-and-white'. It would not give as much information, either, since it could not show the colours of things. Books printed in colour use four inks, each containing strongly coloured chemicals. The ink colours are magenta (pinky-red), cyan (blue), yellow, and black. Coloured photographs and drawings are made up of tiny dots, each dot being one of these four colours. Your eyes 'mix' these dots to give smooth areas of colour. You can see the dots if you look at the pictures with a magnifying glass. Try mixing coloured chemicals yourself, using your paint box.

▲ Paper is bleached before use.

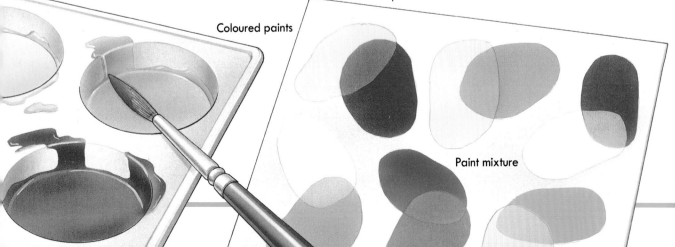

Coloured paints

Paint mixture

Invisible Ink

A simple chemical reaction makes invisible ink visible. Squeeze some juice from a fresh lemon, then write, or paint it onto a piece of white paper. When the juice dries, your marks will be virtually invisible. To make them visible, ask a grown-up to put the paper in an oven at 175°C (gas mark 4) for 10 minutes.

How it works: The heat 'burns' the chemical so it becomes visible.

Fresh lemon juice

Make a Space Meal!

We identify foods by their colour, as well as their smell and taste. Peas are green, lemons are yellow, and oranges are—orange. You can trick your senses by using food colourings to alter ordinary foods, such as baked beans and eggs. Food colourings are chemicals which have a strong colour and which have also been tested thoroughly to make sure they are safe to eat. Add a few drops of colouring to each food, to turn it a strange and unfamiliar colour.

Green drink!

Red lemon!

Blue ice-cubes!

Purple baked beans!

Blue scrambled egg!

Changing States

In science, the **state** of a substance means whether it is solid, liquid or gas. The same chemical can exist in each of these states, depending on its temperature and the pressure on it. A familiar example is water. When very cold, it is solid ice. Normally, it is liquid water. When hot, it is gaseous water vapour. Can you think of other common chemicals that change state?

Solid, Liquid, Gas

In a solid, the atoms or molecules of the substance are arranged in a certain pattern and cannot move. In a liquid, the pattern of arrangement has broken down. The molecules are free to move, but they still stay near each other because they attract each other, like a magnet attracts iron. In a gas, the molecules are much farther apart, too far to attract each other. The 'crazy string' used at parties changes states as you squirt it out. Inside the can it is in liquid form, under high pressure.

How it works: As it squirts out, the pressure is released, and the liquid comes into contact with the air. It changes into a bendy, stringy, plastic solid.

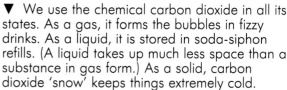

▼ We use the chemical carbon dioxide in all its states. As a gas, it forms the bubbles in fizzy drinks. As a liquid, it is stored in soda-siphon refills. (A liquid takes up much less space than a substance in gas form.) As a solid, carbon dioxide 'snow' keeps things extremely cold.

Skating On Water, Not Ice

Pressure of skate blades on ice melts it into water.

One way to turn a solid to a liquid is by heating it. If you warm ice, it changes to liquid water. We call this 'melting'. Ice changes to water at 0°C. This is its melting point. Solid carbon dioxide has a melting point of minus 78.5°C. Another way to turn a solid to a liquid is to increase its pressure. Put ice under great pressure and it melts into water, because the pressure causes its temperature to rise. This happens under an ice-skater.

How it works: The skate's narrow blades press on the ice and melt it into a tiny pool of water. The slippery water lets the blades slide past.

Non-Melting Chemicals

To stop chocolate melting too quickly, put a few pieces in the freezer or icebox for a couple of hours. Trick your friends by giving them warm pieces, which have been in the airing cupboard, while you have the cold pieces. The warm pieces soon melt all over their hands, while your pieces stay cool and do not melt. This is because a warm piece of chocolate needs only a small amount of heat, which it takes from the hands, to raise its temperature to melting point. A very cold piece needs much more heat to make it melt, and this takes longer to pass from your hands to the chocolate.

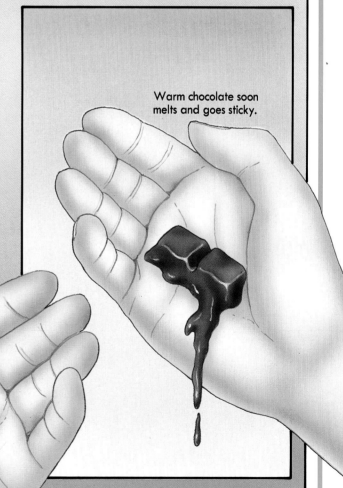

Warm chocolate soon melts and goes sticky.

Ice-cold chocolate stays hard and solid.

Make an Eggshell Fire Extinguisher

Fire involves chemical reactions that need oxygen, a gas in the air (page 96). If there is no oxygen, the fire goes out. Fire blankets and some fire extinguishers work by smothering a fire, to prevent oxygen reaching it.

One substance that can be used for smothering is a gas, carbon dioxide (page 97) You can make a small extinguisher using eggshell and vinegar. Drop small pieces of a clean eggshell into a few teaspoons of vinegar, in a deep container such as a plastic beaker. The ethanoic acid in vinegar reacts with a chemical called calcium carbonate in the shell, to make carbon dioxide gas. This slowly fills the beaker, though you cannot see it. Use it to smother a candle, as shown below.

Equipment: Eggshell, vinegar, plastic beaker, candle.

Carefully pour gas over small lit candle.

Stand candle in sand in deep bowl.

▲ In an emergency, a carbon dioxide (CO_2) fire extinguisher soon smothers a fire and suffocates the flames.

Balloons filled with air containing carbon dioxide – from your lungs!

Collecting Oxygen

Equipment: Pond weed, bowl, jamjar, cotton reels, taper.

Plants and animals make carbon dioxide during their bodily chemical reactions, and plants also make oxygen, by photosynthesis (*page 97*). You can collect these gases as shown here. Use a water plant such as Canadian pondweed, in a bowl or trough of water. Put a large upturned jamjar over it, supported by cotton reels. The plant must be in full sunlight for the best effect. Over a few hours, bubbles of gas form on its leaves and float up to collect in the jamjar. Are they carbon dioxide or oxygen? Carefully lift the jamjar, turn it over, and ask a grown-up to put a long, lighted taper into it. Carbon dioxide will smother the flame. Oxygen will make it burn more brightly.

Gas bubbles collect in jamjar.

Upturned jamjar

Canadian pondweed (or similar waterweed)

Glass or plastic trough

Clean water

Cotton reels

Weed in water

Un-Freezeable Water

Pure water changes from a liquid to solid as its temperature falls below 0°C. We call this freezing. But water that contains a dissolved chemical, such as salt, freezes at a lower temperature. You can make 'un-freezeable water' by dissolving as much salt as you can in cold tap water. Put this salt solution in one plastic container, and clean water in a similar container. Place them in the icebox or freezer. The pure water soon turns to solid ice. The salty water stays liquid for much longer. In very cold weather, salt is spread on roads. It dissolves in any water there, to stop dangerous ice forming on the road surface.

▶ The water in an iceberg freezes at 0°C since it is made from rain water. Sea water freezes well below 0°C, because of the salt dissolved in it.

Mixing Water and Oil—Eventually

Water and cooking oil are both liquids. But they are very different chemicals. It is difficult even to mix them thoroughly. This experiment shows that they can be mixed, eventually, with the help of another liquid chemical—washing-up detergent.

Equipment: Cooking oil, water, glass jars, washing-up liquid.

Water and oil do not mix because their molecules are different. A molecule of water has two atoms of hydrogen and one of oxygen, written H_2O. But a molecule of oil is made of dozens or hundreds of atoms, and contains carbon as well as hydrogen and oxygen. If you shake oil and water together, the oil splits into small globules, but it does not truly dissolve. This mixture, of tiny blobs of one liquid floating in another liquid, is called an **emulsion**. Detergents help to change the oil molecules so that the oil blobs split up even further. They become so small that the oil seems to 'dissolve' in the water.

Cooking oil

Pour oil gently onto water.

1

2

Oil

Water

▲ Put about 5 cm (2 inches) of water in a narrow clear jar or bottle. Carefully add the same amount of oil (1). This soon settles out separately and floats on the water (2).

How Pepper Walks on Water

The surface of a liquid, where it touches the air, has special chemical properties. One of these is surface tension, which creates a kind of 'skin' on the liquid. To show water's skin, put some tap water into a clean plate or shallow tray. Sprinkle pepper grains from a pepper-pot evenly onto the surface. The grains float and stay still on the surface. Gently touch the water with a bar of soap. At once, the pepper grains should float away from the soap and collect around the edges of the container.

How it works: Soap changes the surface tension. The grains are pulled away by the surface tension around the sides.

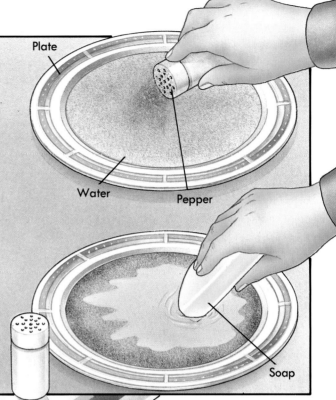

Plate

Water   Pepper

Soap

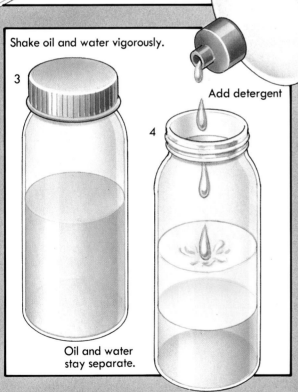

Shake oil and water vigorously.

3

Add detergent

4

Oil and water stay separate.

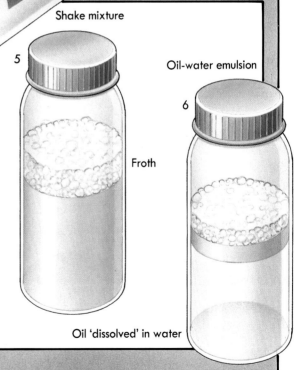

Shake mixture

5

Oil-water emulsion

6

Froth

Oil 'dissolved' in water

▲ Put a top on the jar and carefully shake it. The oil breaks into tiny blobs to form a milky mixture (3). But in an hour, it settles on the water again. Add a few drops of detergent (4).

▲ Shake the jar once more, and a milky liquid forms (5). This has a frothy top, a layer of yellowish milky liquid, and—eventually—a layer of oil 'dissolved' in water (6).

Metals

Some of the most familiar chemicals are metals. Iron, aluminium, lead and steel are all types of metals. The first three of these are also elements (*page 96*). Steel is a combination of iron with small amounts of other substances, such as carbon. Most metals are hard, shiny, strong and carry electricity. They are an essential part of our modern world, used to make hundreds of machines.

The World of Metals

Iron, chemical symbol Fe, is one of the most common elements in the Earth's rocks. We see iron as a hard metal that is fashioned into kitchen utensils, railings, gates and girders. Yet deep inside the Earth, where temperatures and pressures are enormous, there are vast amounts of liquid iron.

Aluminium, symbol Al, is even more common than iron. It makes up about one-twelfth of the Earth's surface. It is very light, used to make parts for planes and high-speed cars and trains.

Lead, symbol Pb, is one of the heaviest and softest metals. In former times lead was beaten into sheets for roofs and bent into pipes for water. However we now know that lead is poisonous to the human body, even in tiny amounts.

Titanium, symbol Ti, is another very common metal in the Earth's rocks. But it is difficult to obtain in its pure form. Strong as steel, and half the weight, it is used in jet engines.

Copper, symbol Cu, is a reddish metal that carries electricity very well. It is suited to making electrical wires and cables. Also it does not rust, and has taken over from lead in water pipes.

Alloys are combinations of metals. Bronze is an alloy of copper and tin. Brass is an alloy of copper and zinc.

Metals Around the Home

Look around your home or school. Can you spot things that are made of metals? Some are shown below. Each type of metal is chosen for hardness and strength, to suit its job, from a paper clip to a carving blade. Most metals are found in nature in rocks, combined with many other chemicals. They must first be extracted, which means obtaining them in a pure form. Then they are heated to make them melt, and poured into moulds.

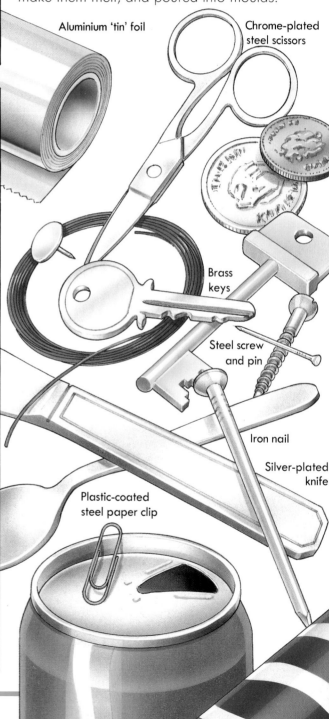

Aluminium 'tin' foil

Chrome-plated steel scissors

Brass keys

Steel screw and pin

Iron nail

Silver-plated knife

Plastic-coated steel paper clip

Sorting Metals

Only the metal iron can be magnetized, to make a permanent magnet. An iron magnet attracts other substances that are made of iron or contain iron (such as steel). Discover which objects contain iron by putting a bar magnet near them. Nails, needles and pins are usually made of steel, and they stick to a magnet. Other items are made of iron but then coated with another metal. A 'brass' drawing pin may be made of steel, with a thin layer of brass on top.

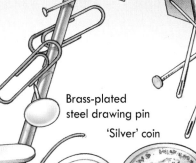

'Copper' coin

Brass-plated
steel drawing pin

'Silver' coin

Copper
electrical wire

Making Metals

Certain metals are heated or 'blasted' in a furnace to extract them from their ores (the rocks that contain them). Iron flows straight from its furnace at a temperature of 1500°C. In some cases the heat is created by passing huge electric currents through the metal, rather like a gigantic electric fire! The rocks melt and the metal separates and floats to the surface.

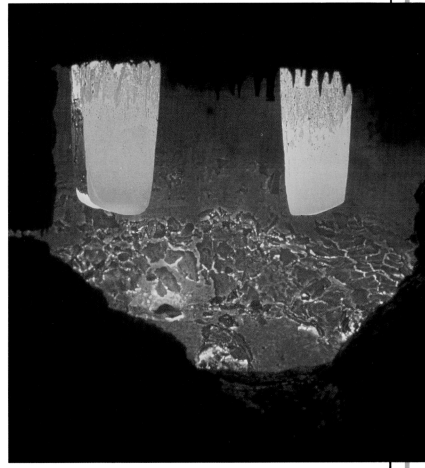

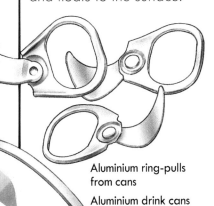

Aluminium ring-pulls
from cans

Aluminium drink cans

Chemical Electricity

Electricity is generated when certain chemicals react together. We use chemically made electricity to power many machines, from a torch to a personal stereo, an electronic quartz watch and the electrical circuits of a car. We usually call these devices 'batteries'. When the chemicals are used up, the electricity stops—unless the battery is rechargeable!

Make a Lemon Battery

A simple battery which produces only a small, safe amount of electricity can be made from a lemon, as shown below. In a battery, there is a central chemical called the **electrolyte**. This is placed between, and in contact with, two other substances, the **electrodes**, which are usually made of metal. When a wire and bulb are added to make an electrical circuit, the chemical reaction between the electrolytes and the electrodes creates electricity. This flows round the circuit and makes the bulb glow. In an ordinary torch battery, or 'dry cell', the electrolyte is ammonium chloride paste. One electrode is a carbon rod in the centre of the battery, with a brass cap. The other is the zinc battery case.

Equipment: Brass drawing pin, paper clip, lemon, torch bulb, electrical wire.

To make the lemon battery, stick a brass drawing pin and a steel paper clip into opposite sides of a fresh lemon. Connect a low-voltage torch bulb (less than 3 volts) by two pieces of electrical wire to make the circuit. The acidic juice of the lemon is the electrolyte. The drawing pin and the paper clip are the two electrodes.

▼ A small battery as used in cameras and watches.

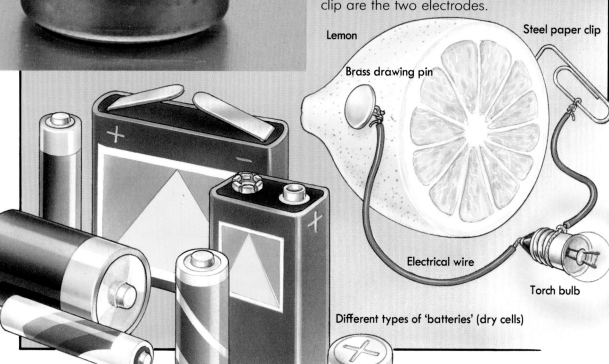

Lemon

Steel paper clip

Brass drawing pin

Electrical wire

Torch bulb

Different types of 'batteries' (dry cells)

Electricity in Industry

Electrical power is vital in today's world, from powering toy trains to real ones. The metal aluminium is obtained in pure form by passing huge amounts of electricity through its refined rock ore in pots, in a process known as **electrolysis** or 'smelting' (*see below*). Each smelting pot uses electrical currents of up to 150,000 amps, and there may be 1000 pots in one refinery. (A normal household plug works on a maximum of 13 amps.) The electricity for this process may well have come originally from another chemical reaction—the burning of coal or oil.

Splitting Up Water

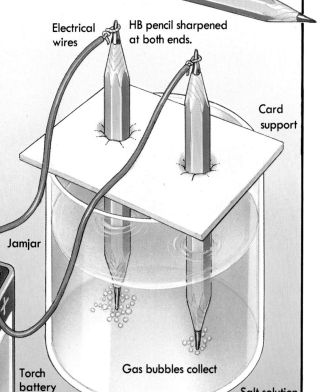

Chemical changes can generate electricity. Electricity can also produce chemical changes. Water is a simple chemical made of hydrogen and oxygen (*page 112*). If an electric current is passed through it, between electrodes, the water is split into its two constituents, hydrogen and oxygen, which are both gases (*see below*). This process, electrolysis, is used in industry in many ways, such as obtaining metals like aluminium (*above*). If one of the electrodes is a metal, it will become covered or 'plated' with any metal in the electrolyte. This is how 'tin' cans are made.

Connect a battery using wires to two HB pencils, which are the electrodes. Place their other ends in water with a little salt dissolved in it, as shown. The electricity splits water into hydrogen and oxygen, which collect as bubbles around each pencil tip.

Equipment: Torch battery, two HB pencils, salt, card, electrical wire.

Electrical wires

HB pencil sharpened at both ends.

Card support

Jamjar

Torch battery

Gas bubbles collect

Salt solution

Carbon Chemistry

Carbon-containing chemicals are the basis of life. Atoms of carbon combine with atoms of other elements, like oxygen, hydrogen and nitrogen, to make the bodies of living things. Every plant and animal, from a daisy to an elephant, has a body whose chemicals are based on carbon. The study of carbon chemicals and how they react is known as **organic chemistry**.

The Power for Life

Living things need energy to power the chemical reactions going on inside their bodies. This energy comes from the Sun. Plants capture the Sun's light energy directly, by photosynthesis (*page 97*). They use some of this energy for living. They also store some in chemical form, as the molecules in their bodies. Animals eat plants and take in the energy-containing molecules. They use some of the energy for their own life processes, and store the rest in their bodies. Other animals eat them, take in the energy, and so on. In this way we can trace the web of life back, to see that the energy for all life comes from the Sun. The Sun's heat warms the Earth and causes winds—another form of energy. In the Sun, the vast amounts of energy are created by a type of massive chemical-nuclear reaction. The Sun will continue to shine for billions of years, before it runs out of energy.

Over millions of years, the Sun's energy has been stored in countless living bodies. By slow chemical reactions, they turned into coal, oil and gas. When we burn these fuels, we release this energy.

Oil and Gas

Coal

Wind and Sun

Toasting Marshmallows

Most of the foods we eat were once living things, either plants or animals. So they contain lots of carbon. Often, when organic chemicals are burned, the carbon changes its form and may be left in its powdery black form. This is why food turns dark or black if it's burnt during cooking.

Ask a grown-up to toast marshmallows safely near a gentle flame. You can see the sugary marshmallows burn slightly, and carbon appears as a dark substance.

Before toasting   After toasting

Turn Milk into Plastic

Equipment: Creamy milk, saucepan, vinegar.

Many plastics are made from petroleum oil. Oil formed in the rocks over millions of years, from the bodies of billions of small sea creatures. You can make a similar 'plastic' in a few minutes—using milk, another organic (carbon-containing) substance.

Ask a grown-up to warm some creamy milk in a saucepan. When it is just simmering, slowly stir in a few teaspoons of vinegar. The acidic chemicals in the vinegar react with the organic milk chemicals. Keep stirring until it becomes rubbery. Let it cool and wash it under running water. You now have your own plastic, which you can bounce around or mould into shapes.

Drip vinegar slowly into warm milk.

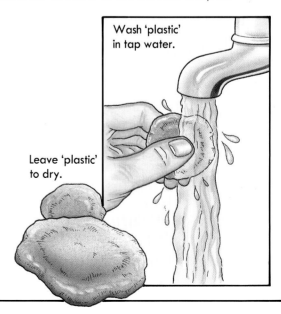

Wash 'plastic' in tap water.

Leave 'plastic' to dry.

Biochemistry

Biochemistry is the study of chemical reactions in living things. Experts have learned much about how biochemical reactions occur and how they are controlled. Living things such as microscopic bacteria can be programmed to act as tiny 'biochemical factories' and make useful substances, such as medicines (*page 125*).

▶ In this fermenting room, useful chemicals are being made biochemically, by microscopic bacteria and yeasts. Cleanliness is vital. Unwanted germs can ruin the reactions.

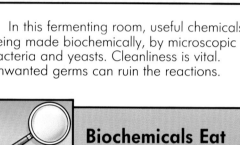

Biochemicals Eat a Boiled Egg!

'Biological' washing powders contain enzymes. Inside a living body, there are thousands of enzymes. They control the speed of biochemical reactions going on in the body. Some enzymes are especially good at splitting up or 'eating' organic substances. In biological washing powder, these types of enzymes attack and dissolve away oil, and dirt stains. Dissolve ordinary washing powder in warm water in a jamjar, and biological powder in another. Put a peeled hard-boiled egg into each jar, and leave them in a warm place for a few days. Enzymes in the biological powder 'eat away' the organic chemicals of the egg, while the other egg is not affected.

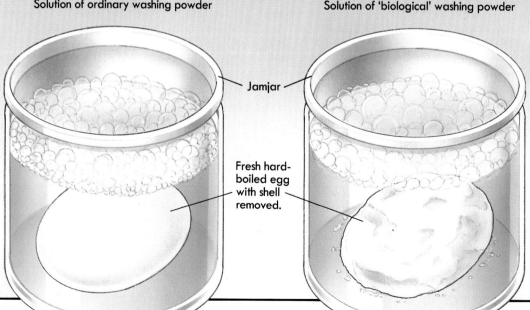

Solution of ordinary washing powder

Solution of 'biological' washing powder

Jamjar

Fresh hard-boiled egg with shell removed.

The Conditions for Life

Living things need certain conditions in order to grow and flourish. They need a supply of oxygen, the right temperature, and the right amounts of moisture. These conditions allow the biochemical reactions of life to continue inside their bodies. Each plant and animal is suited to particular conditions. A waterweed needs to be in water and a mouse must be in air, or they will die.

Dry cotton wool

Moist cotton wool

Soaking-wet cotton wool

Even small changes in the chemical conditions surrounding a plant or animal, can cause problems. This simple experiment grows cress seeds under different conditions. You need three plastic jamjar lids. Put a layer of cotton wool into each, and sprinkle on a few cress seeds. Place them in a warm, light, airy place. Keep the cotton wool dry in one lid, damp in the second, and wet in the third. Which grows best?

Chemicals in the Body

Like everything in the world, the human body is made up of chemicals. And like all living things, you are made mainly of organic chemicals such as proteins, fats and carbohydrates (*page 123*). These are based mainly on the elements carbon, hydrogen and oxygen. However, the chemical reactions for life cannot happen unless these organic molecules are free to move about, mix and react together. To do this, they must be dissolved or floating in water. This is why there is so much water in the body. In fact, you are almost two-thirds water!

Water 65%

Protein 18%

Fat 10%

Carbohydrate 5%

Others 2%

Recipe for the Body

The diagram above shows the proportions of some of the main chemicals in the body. There are also dozens of other chemicals, present in smaller amounts. They include iron for your blood, sodium and potassium for your nerves, calcium for your bones and teeth, and phosphorus for turning energy into movement.

The Chemicals in Food

When we mention 'chemicals' in food, people may imagine the artificial colourings and flavourings made in a chemical factory. But food is made up of many other natural chemicals, that are part of the plants and animals it is made from. To stay healthy, your body needs the right proportions of three main types of food chemicals. Carbohydrates are found in sugary and starchy foods, such as bread, fruits and vegetables. They are the main energy-providers for the body. Fats and oils occur in dairy products, fatty meats and oily foods. They are used to make certain parts of cells. Proteins are contained in meat, fish, dairy products, fruits and vegetables. They provide most of the building materials for the body, for growth and repairing wear-and-tear.

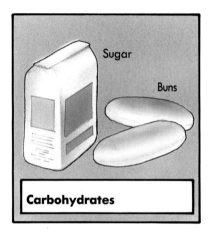

Carbohydrates

Fats and Oils

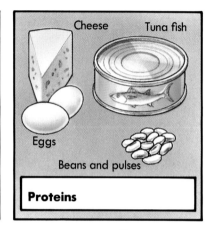

Proteins

Making Caramel

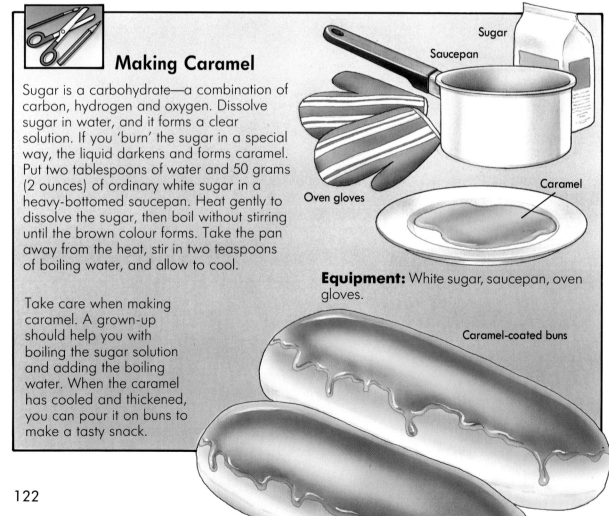

Sugar is a carbohydrate—a combination of carbon, hydrogen and oxygen. Dissolve sugar in water, and it forms a clear solution. If you 'burn' the sugar in a special way, the liquid darkens and forms caramel. Put two tablespoons of water and 50 grams (2 ounces) of ordinary white sugar in a heavy-bottomed saucepan. Heat gently to dissolve the sugar, then boil without stirring until the brown colour forms. Take the pan away from the heat, stir in two teaspoons of boiling water, and allow to cool.

Take care when making caramel. A grown-up should help you with boiling the sugar solution and adding the boiling water. When the caramel has cooled and thickened, you can pour it on buns to make a tasty snack.

Equipment: White sugar, saucepan, oven gloves.

Soda Bread

Normal bread uses the biochemical reactions in yeast, to produce the carbon dioxide gas which makes it 'rise' (see *below*). In soda bread, a chemical reaction between baking soda, sugar, buttermilk and other ingredients produces carbon dioxide bubbles in the soft dough. As the dough is heated further, it sets like a sponge.

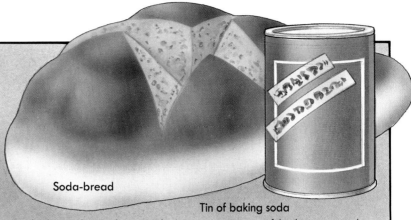

Soda-bread

Tin of baking soda

Soda bread can be made at home, with the help of a grown-up. Find the recipe in a good cookery book, and follow it carefully. It is important to add the exact amounts of baking powder and bicarbonate of soda. Too little, and the bread will not rise when baked. Too much, and it will bubble up quickly and then collapse.

Wine and Bread

Yeast consists of tiny living cells, related to mushrooms. As they 'breathe' they make carbon dioxide gas. To make bread, yeast cells are mixed into the dough. The cells create bubbles of carbon dioxide gas, which puff up the dough and make it rise. Yeast cells also make alcohol as a by-product.

Block of dried, pressed yeast

Cheeses and Yoghurts

Cheese is made by a two-stage chemical change. The first involves milk and rennet. This is an enzyme found in calves' stomachs. Rennet digests or 'curdles' the milk and makes it partly solid. The curdled milk is warmed, squeezed, shaped into blocks and stored. During this time bacteria turn it into ripe cheese or yoghurt.

Cheese and yoghurt

The Chemical Industry

In olden times, people's needs were simple. They used natural materials and ate fresh foods, or foods stored by drying or salting. Today we have invented any number of unnatural, man-made chemicals that are used to manufacture cars, planes, stereo systems, toys, buildings, furniture and machinery. Our food has chemicals added. The chemical industry's products are a major part of everyday life.

► ▼ A giant refinery (right) makes dozens of chemicals out of crude oil from petrol for cars to asphalt on roads. A robot (below) paints a new car.

Robot arm

124

Agrichemicals

Farmers rely more and more on artificial chemicals to grow their crops. Man-made fertilizers are added to the soil, to improve yield. Seeds are coated with fungicides when they are stored, to stop them going bad. The soil is sprayed with herbicides, which kill the unwanted plants we call 'weeds'. Growing crops are sprayed with pesticides, to stop insects and other pests from damaging them.

▶ A sprayer soaks the growing crops with a cocktail of chemicals, designed to kill pests and stop diseases.

Biochemicals

The biochemical industry has made enormous progress in recent years. Bacteria and other microscopic organisms (page 120) can be altered to manufacture the chemicals we need. In former times, many medicines were extracted from animals and plants. These medicines could be difficult to obtain, and expensive. Experts in biotechnology can now produce some of these medicines in 'fermenting vats'. Insulin, a hormonal medicine needed by people with the disease diabetes, was purified from the leftover carcases of cows and pigs. Human-type insulin can now be made in a fermenting vat.

◀ Biotechnologists and biochemists work to develop new ways of manufacturing medicines, drugs and food ingredients.

Waste Chemicals

The chemical business is big business. Huge amounts of money and many thousands of jobs are involved. But chemicals, especially waste chemicals, are damaging our world. They are soaking into the water, seeping through the land, and spreading into the air. How will they change the world? For example, we are discovering that chlorofluorocarbons (CFCs), chemicals used in some aerosols, are damaging the ozone layer around the Earth. Dozens of other chemicals might cause similar problems in the future. No one can be sure how these substances will affect our land, sea and air.

Damaging waste chemicals take many forms. Some are radioactive. Used-up fuels, protective clothing and equipment from nuclear power stations give off radiation that could damage life and cause disease. The radiation may last for thousands of years in some cases. No one knows how to deal with these chemicals and make them safe. At present, we are storing them as best we can.

▲ More and more people are becoming aware of the dangers from waste chemicals. This is especially so when the chemicals are not disposed of properly.

SOS: Things To Do

We can start a Save Our Surroundings by being careful with chemicals, of all kinds.
- Buy only what you need. A seemingly harmless product, like a little plastic toy, needs energy and raw materials to make it.
- Check before buying. Chemicals which do not damage the surroundings too much are usually labelled 'environment-friendly' or similar. This is particularly important for strong chemicals such as detergents and cleaners.
- Use chemicals carefully. Do not buy more than you need, letting the rest go bad. Store chemicals safely. Dispose of them according to the instructions. If you do not need all you have bought, sell or give away the rest.
- Recycle chemicals. Collect glass, paper, aluminium and other substances so that they can be re-used (see *opposite*). Buy things made from recycled chemicals if you can.
- Help to save the environment. Join an organization that does practical work such as recycling or cleaning up natural areas.

◀ ▼ Keep the countryside tidy. Waste and litter are not only unsightly, they are also a danger to wildlife and a waste of natural materials. We cannot go on wasting chemicals for ever. Supplies will run out.

Aluminium cans

Papers

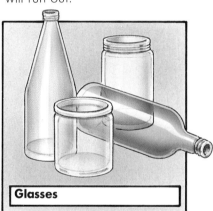

Glasses

Recycling

It is extremely wasteful to extract huge quantities of raw materials from the Earth, only to throw them away, little changed, after use. Many substances can be re-used and recycled, to save both materials and money. Have your own 'recycling bins' at home, and visit the bottle bank or paper-collection point often.

Galvanized steel cans

Plastics

Simple Chemistry Quiz

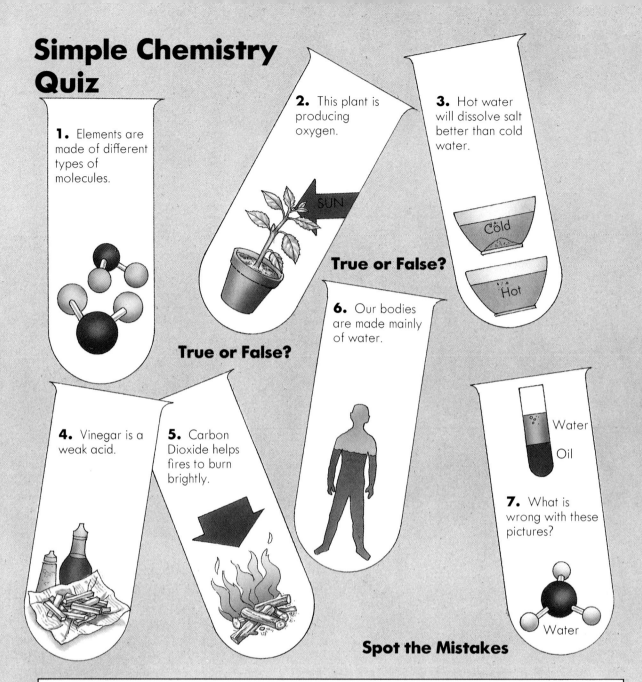

1. Elements are made of different types of molecules.

2. This plant is producing oxygen.

SUN

True or False?

3. Hot water will dissolve salt better than cold water.

Cold

Hot

True or False?

6. Our bodies are made mainly of water.

4. Vinegar is a weak acid.

5. Carbon Dioxide helps fires to burn brightly.

Water

Oil

7. What is wrong with these pictures?

Water

Spot the Mistakes

Answers

1. False. All elements are made of only one kind of molecule (page 96).

2. True. During the day plants use photosynthesis to make food and produce oxygen (page 111).

3. True. Hot water can 'hold' more dissolved substances than cold water (page 99).

4. True. Acids such as vinegar have sharp tastes. lemon juice is also acidic (page 104).

5. False. Carbon Dioxide will put out a fire. Flames need oxygen to burn brightly (page 110).

6. True. The human body is about two thirds water (page 121).

7. Top: Oil will always float on water because it is less dense (page 112).
Bottom: A water molecule is made up of one oxygen atom and two, not three, hydrogen atoms (page 96).

WEATHER

This section of the book will help you to investigate the weather. Think about the weather every time you go outside. Think about the clouds and the wind or whether it is hot or cold.

There are six main topics in this section:

- Atmosphere, air, temperature and wind
- Days and seasons; wind and water currents around the globe
- Moisture in the air, humidity, clouds, rain, snow and hail
- Thunder and lightning, rainbows and mirages
- Weather forecasts and weather maps
- How weather shapes the land and affects animals, plants and people

Use the symbols below to help you identify the three kinds of practical activities in this book.

EXPERIMENTS

TRICKS

THINGS TO MAKE

Introduction

The first part of this section tells you about the features of our ever-changing weather, such as temperature, winds, clouds, and storms. The middle part shows how weather is measured, and how weather forecasts are made. The last part looks at how the weather affects us – and how we might be affecting the weather.

Throughout the section, there are simple and safe experiments, projects and tricks which you can carry out. The questions on these two pages are based on the scientific ideas explained in this section. As you carry out the experiments, you should be able to answer these questions, and understand more about the weather and how it affects the world around us.

▲ How far away is a thunderstorm? (pages 152–153)

▼ What are 'all the colours of the rainbow', and how can you make them for yourself? (page 154)

▼ How does the weather help us to design our homes and buildings? (page 163)

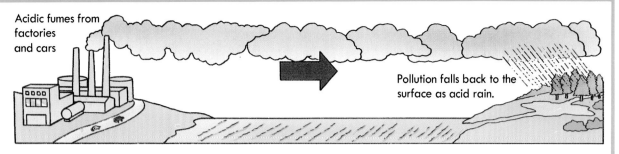

Acidic fumes from factories and cars

Pollution falls back to the surface as acid rain.

▲ Are we changing the weather? How will this affect our world? (pages 166–167)

▲ How do experts predict the weather? And how often are they right? (pages 156–159)

▶ What is wind, and how do we measure it? (pages 138–143)

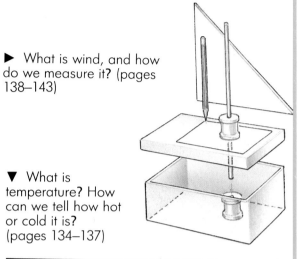

▼ What is temperature? How can we tell how hot or cold it is? (pages 134–137)

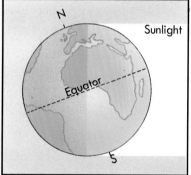

Sunlight

Equator

◀ How does the Earth's place in space make day and night? (page 136)

▼ Where does rain come from, and how can you tell the amount that falls? (pages 144–149)

▶ How does the climate affect where plants and animals live? (pages 162–165)

An Ocean of Air

It is all around us, but cannot be seen. We can only feel it when it blows on our faces. We can only hear it as it rustles the trees and whistles past buildings. Yet we need to breathe it, or we will die. It is air. Our world is covered with air, called the **atmosphere**. The Earth's gravity keeps it near its surface. Otherwise our spinning planet would fling it off into space.

The Atmosphere

The air in our atmosphere is made of a mixture of colourless gases. These are mainly nitrogen (almost four-fifths), oxygen (one-fifth), plus many other gases, such as argon and carbon dioxide, in tiny amounts.

The air in the atmosphere is densest, or 'thickest', near the ground. As we travel higher it becomes thinner, or more rarefied.

You can feel the weight of air by spreading a large sheet of newspaper flat on a table, and sliding a ruler under one side, as shown below. Hit the ruler hard. It is difficult to lift the paper, because of the weight of air pressing on it. This is called air pressure, and it pushes down at about 1 kilogram per square centimetre.

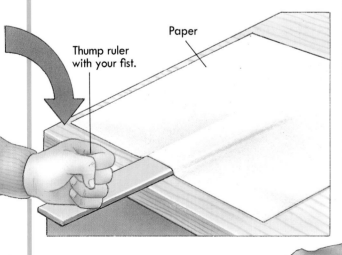

Paper

Thump ruler with your fist.

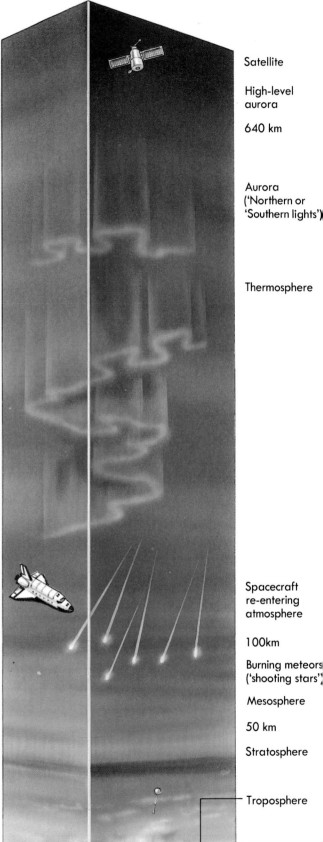

Satellite

High-level aurora

640 km

Aurora ('Northern or 'Southern lights')

Thermosphere

Spacecraft re-entering atmosphere

100km

Burning meteors ('shooting stars')

Mesosphere

50 km

Stratosphere

Troposphere

Using Air to Hold up Water

Air presses in all directions as this trick shows. Fill a clean beaker to the brim with water. Press a square piece of strong card on top to make a good seal. Keeping the beaker over the sink, very carefully turn it over . . . and the water should stay inside!

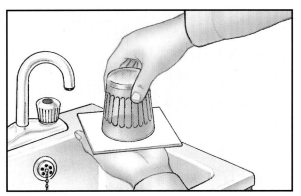

Air pushes upwards on card and keeps water in.

How it works: Air is pressing upwards on the card with enough force to hold the water in place. Push down gently on the corner of the card to break the seal, and air bubbles in it. It now presses downwards as well as up. The card falls away, and the water pours out.

Balancing Balloons!

Air, like most substances, becomes bigger (**expands**) as it is heated. Show that a certain volume of hot air weighs less than the same volume of cold air, by a 'balloon balance'. Blow up two balloons to the same size. Tie each balloon to one end of a long, thin piece of wood (such as a dowel or garden cane). Balance this on a pencil supported by cans or books, and mark the balance point on the wood.

Saucepan   Balloon

Tip: The balloons are the same size when they touch the saucepan's side.

Next, put one balloon in a cold place such as the fridge, and the other in a warm place like the airing cupboard. Let some air out of the warm balloon and blow some air into the cold balloon, so that they are the same size. Now do they balance?

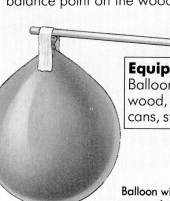

Equipment:
Balloons, piece of wood, pencil, cans, sticky tape.

Balloon with warm air

Balloon with cold air

Testing the Temperature

Air temperature is the 'hotness' or 'coldness' of the air. This is measured by an instrument known as a thermometer.

A scale on the thermometer shows the temperature, which is usually measured in degrees Celsius, written °C. Weather experts use different types of thermometers for different jobs.

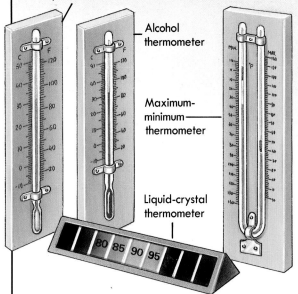

Mercury thermometer

Alcohol thermometer

Maximum-minimum thermometer

Liquid-crystal thermometer

▲ A Campbell-Stokes sunshine recorder. The Sun's rays burn a line on a paper chart. Its length shows hours of sunlight.

◄ An alcohol thermometer is used in very cold places, as the usual mercury freezes at minus 39°C.

In the summer
You can record air temperatures with a thermometer on a shady wall, out of direct sunlight. The temperature on a hot summer day is 25–30°C.

In the winter
In winter the average temperatures are much lower. Water freezes at 0°C. When the air temperature falls below this for a time, ponds and lakes ice over.

Heat from the Sun

The Sun gives out rays of various types. We can see one type – these are light rays, or sunlight. The Sun also gives out heat, in the form of infra-red rays.

How it works: Smooth, shiny surfaces reflect both light and heat rays. Dull, roughened surfaces absorb them.

A simple experiment reveals the power of the Sun to warm different substances by different amounts.

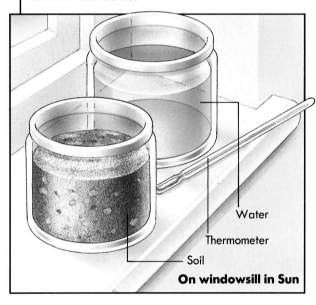

Water
Thermometer
Soil
On windowsill in Sun

▲ In hot places, people wear loose, light coloured clothes. The light colour reflects the Sun's heat, keeping the person cool.

> **Equipment:** Identical glass jars, soil, thermometer, water.

You need two identical glass jars. Carefully half-fill one with dark, fairly dry soil and the other with water. Put them on a sunny window ledge (*above left*), and measure their temperatures straight away with a standard mercury thermometer. (Take extra care, mercury is poisonous.)

Measure their temperatures again after half an hour and one hour. The dark soil absorbs the Sun's heat more quickly than the 'shiny' water and so warms up more rapidly. Now place both jars in a shady place indoors, under a dark cloth (*below left*). Which one cools down more quickly?

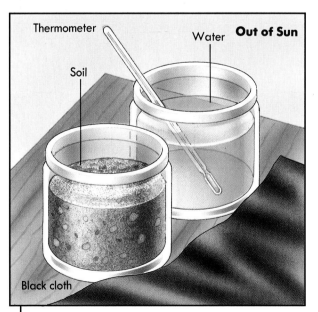

Thermometer
Water **Out of Sun**
Soil
Black cloth

Where's Warmest and Coldest?

The world's hottest place is Dallol, Ethiopia. Average temperatures over several years were 34.4°C (94°F). Coldest is on Antarctica, where the average temperatures are minus 55°C (minus 70°F)!

Days and Seasons

Planet Earth's movements in space produce the regular changes of day and night, and summer and winter. The planets circle a star, which we call the Sun. It takes one year for the Earth to make a complete circuit. The Earth also spins around itself, once each day.

Summer and Winter, Day and Night

The Earth is not at right angles to the Sun. It is tilted slightly. On its yearly journey around the Sun, the upper part of the Earth (the North) is nearer to the Sun for a few months. The Sun's rays pass almost straight down through the atmosphere, so less of their energy is lost in the atmosphere, and more reaches the surface. It is summer in the North.

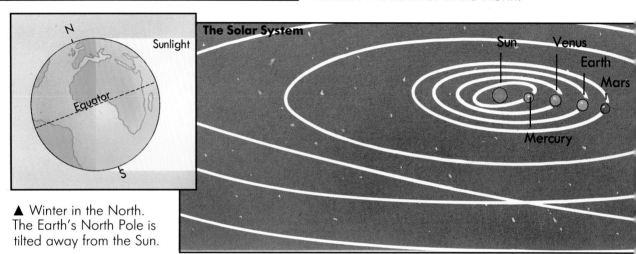

▲ Winter in the North. The Earth's North Pole is tilted away from the Sun.

The Solar System

Sun · Venus · Earth · Mars · Mercury

Make a Garden Sundial

You can use the Sun to tell the time, by making a sundial, as shown on the right. Cover a board or large book with white paper for a base. Make a right-angled triangle of card about 15 centimetres (6 inches) at the base, with a flap at the bottom. Stick the flap on the base, using cotton guy ropes if necessary to keep it upright. Draw two curved lines from the corners of the base to the triangle's high side.

Place the sundial where it will get the Sun for most of the day. Use a compass to make the tall vertical side of the triangle point North. Through the day, as the Sun moves it casts a shadow from the card. With a watch to tell the time, mark and label the shadow's position each hour, where it crosses the curved lines. Next day, you can use the sundial to tell the time – provided it is sunny!

Equipment: Compass, card, heavy base.

20 cms
15 cms
15 cms → Fold

Card triangle points North.

Mark position of shadow hourly.

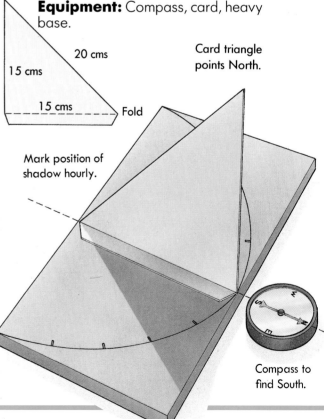

Compass to find South.

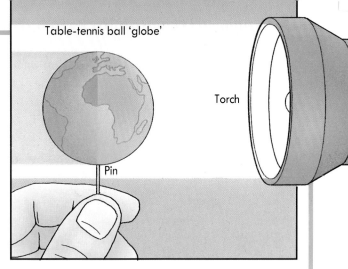
Table-tennis ball 'globe'

Torch

Pin

Meanwhile, the lower part of the Earth (the South) is farther from the Sun. The rays pass at a slanting angle through the atmosphere, where much of their energy is absorbed. It is winter in the South. As the Earth reaches the opposite side of its circle around the Sun, the seasons are reversed.

Draw a simple world map on a table-tennis ball. Carefully stick this on a pin, and shine a narrow-beam torch from the side. Twirl the ball slowly to show how day and night happen. Can you see why, on Earth, the Sun seems to travel across the sky?

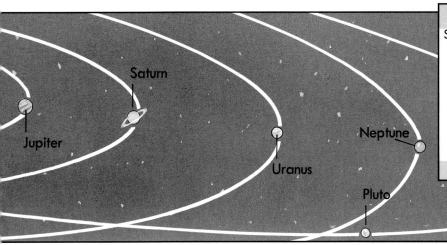

Saturn

Jupiter

Neptune

Uranus

Pluto

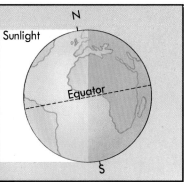
Sunlight

N

Equator

S

▲ Winter in the South. The Earth's South Pole is tilted away from the Sun.

▶ The Sun's light and heat rays are a powerful source of energy. Solar panels capture this energy and turn it into electricity. The car *Sunraycer* won a race across Australia, powered only by the Sun. Solar power will be important in the future, since it causes little pollution and the Sun will last for billions of years.

Where's the Hottest?

The highest temperature ever recorded was in Libya. The temperature was 58°C (136°F). And that was in the shade, which is the standard way to read the air temperature. In the sun it was hotter!

Measuring the Way the Wind Blows

When we say 'a north wind' we refer to the direction the wind blows from, not where it blows to. You can make a wind recorder (*right*) to measure the wind's direction.

Put a length of dowel through two cotton reels so that it spins easily. Glue one reel into the base of a shoebox, the other on the lid directly above, with a hole in the lid for the dowel. Tape a piece of paper to the lid, for the recording chart. Make a wind vane from a triangle of card, and fix a soft-lead pencil (6B) to its upright edge. Tape the middle of the vane to the dowel, so that as it spins the pencil draws a line on the recording chart. Place the wind recorder in an exposed place, steadied by stones in the shoebox. Draw a North–South line on the recording chart. As the wind changes direction, the pencil traces a line on the chart. The thickest part of the line shows where the wind has been blowing from for most of the time.

Equipment: Shoebox, two cotton reels, about 35 centimetres (14 inches) of dowel to fit in the reels, compass, 6B pencil, paper, glue, triangle of strong card, sticky tape.

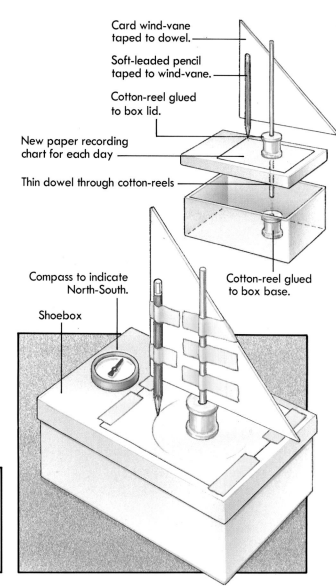

Card wind-vane taped to dowel.

Soft-leaded pencil taped to wind-vane.

Cotton-reel glued to box lid.

New paper recording chart for each day

Thin dowel through cotton-reels

Compass to indicate North-South.

Shoebox

Cotton-reel glued to box base.

The World's Winds

The Sun's heat energy warms different parts of the atmosphere by day and by night, and through the seasons. This keeps our weather on the move. Warm air is lighter than cold air and rises (*see page 133*). Cold air flows in to take its place. These movements create large-scale wind patterns or 'wind belts' around the world.

There are Polar Easterlies, Trades, and Prevailing Westerlies. Along the Equator is a region where winds seldom blow, the Doldrums.

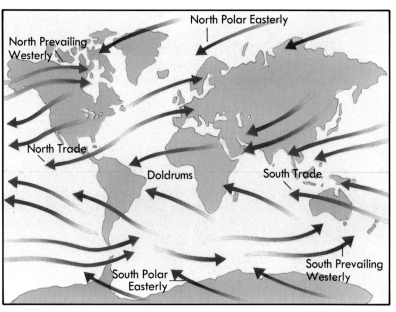

North Polar Easterly

North Prevailing Westerly

North Trade

Doldrums

South Trade

South Polar Easterly

South Prevailing Westerly

Water – Warm and Cold

Just as the Sun warms the atmosphere and creates winds, so it warms the surface of the oceans and helps to create water currents. You can demonstrate that cold water is heavier, or more dense, than warm water in your own bathtub!

Put a few drops of food colouring in a plastic bottle. Fill this with cold water and shake it to colour the water evenly. Screw on the top and place the bottle in the fridge for a few hours so that the water becomes even colder. Half fill the bath with warm water. Place the plastic bottle on the bottom. Carefully unscrew the top so that the cold, coloured water seeps out slowly. Watch how this cold, dense water spreads out – but stays near the bottom of the bath.

How it works: Cold water is denser, or heavier than warm water and sinks to the bottom.

Equipment:

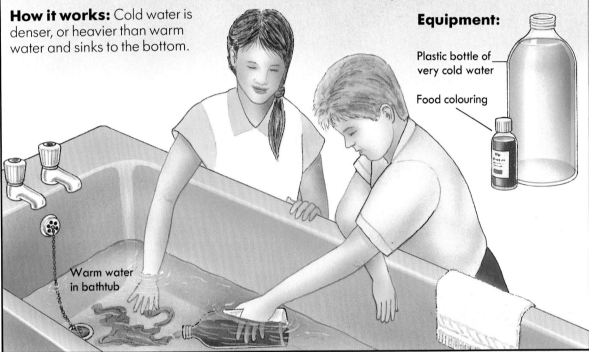

Warm water in bathtub

Plastic bottle of very cold water

Food colouring

The World's Currents

The Sun's warmth and the winds, plus the spinning of the Earth and the tidal pull of the Moon and Sun combine to create oceanic water currents. The currents also change direction to flow around the great land masses.

These currents affect our weather, and they carry vast amounts of water. The West Wind Drift, which flows westwards around Antarctica, transports more than 200 times the amount of water carried by the Amazon.

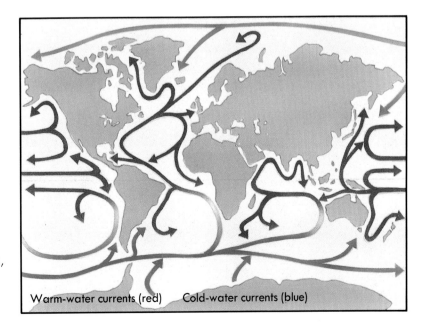

Warm-water currents (red)   Cold-water currents (blue)

Power from the Wind

We can capture the Sun's energy directly, as light and/or heat (*solar power, see page 137*). We can also capture it indirectly from the weather, by harnessing the power of the winds it creates. Like solar power, wind power produces little pollution, and it will be available as long as the Sun itself lasts.

Some people say that rows of huge windmills are a form of 'visual pollution'.

To make a windmill carefully cut four vanes in a star shape from stiff card, as shown below. Fold back a strip along one edge, on the same side, of each vane. Fix the star to a piece of dowel or cane, with a drawing pin through its centre, so that it is free to turn. Hold the windmill facing into a good stiff breeze, and it should spin rapidly. What happens if you fold the strips on each vane forwards instead of backwards?

▲▼ Windmills have been used for centuries (*above*), to grind wheat into flour, pump water and do other tasks. The modern version (*below*) converts wind power into electricity.

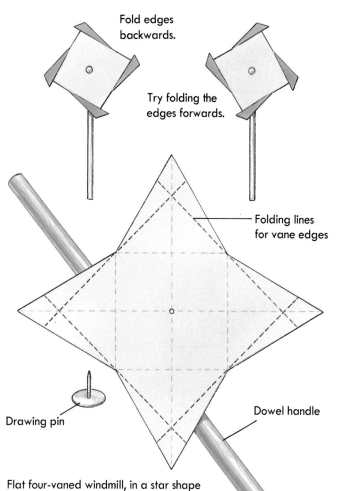

Fold edges backwards.

Try folding the edges forwards.

Folding lines for vane edges

Drawing pin

Dowel handle

Flat four-vaned windmill, in a star shape

Put a Sock in the Wind!

Windsocks are used at airports, sea ports and other exposed places such as mountain roads (*right*). The sock swivels away from the wind, which then blows into its open end or 'mouth'. The sock's tail points the way the wind is blowing. A stiff sock means a strong wind. If it flops loosely, the wind is only light. You can make a windsock using the instructions below.

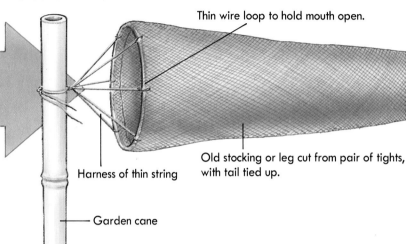

Thin wire loop to hold mouth open.

WIND

Harness of thin string

Old stocking or leg cut from pair of tights, with tail tied up.

Garden cane

Where is Windiest?

The strongest wind was 371 kilometres per hour on Mount Washington, in eastern North America.

Winds in the Great Gale in South-East England, October 1987 gusted to 160 kilometres per hour.

Bubbles Blowing in the Wind

Equipment: Bubble-blowing kit.
Care: No bubbles near busy roads!

Most winds blow in one direction. On a local scale, this can vary with features such as hills, trees and buildings, that make the wind change direction and slow down or speed up. Reveal local wind patterns by blowing bubbles outside on a windy day. Watch them go round or over obstacles.

The Devastating Hurricane

A hurricane is formed when strong winds blow into an area of low air pressure (see *page 158*), and swirl violently in a circle. They develop over the warm tropical waters of the Atlantic Ocean, in the summer. Similar storms are called cyclones in the Indian Ocean, and typhoons in the Pacific.

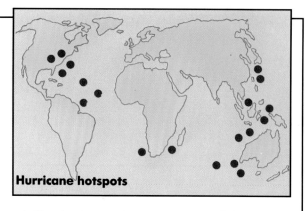

Hurricane hotspots

▲ Tropical storm hot-spots around the world. Where they hit the land, the strong winds do immense damage.

Hurricane

◄ Average wind speeds in a hurricane are at least 120 kilometres per hour (74 miles per hour). Yet in the 'eye' at the centre, there is hardly any wind at all.

▼ A satellite photograph of a hurricane over the Gulf of Mexico. The dashed lines show the coast. A computer has colour-coded the scene, with the strongest winds in red.

How Fast is the Wind Blowing?

With the help of an adult, you can make an **anemometer** to measure how fast the wind blows, as shown here.

Bend a loop at the end of a length of stiff wire. File the other end flat. Tape the loop to the bottom of a shoebox. Put stones in the box to steady it, and place the lid on, making a hole for the wire. Tape two thin pieces of wood into a cross. Push four paper cups onto the ends of the wood, facing in a circle. Securely fix the centre of the cross to the end (top) of an empty ballpoint pen tube with a

Equipment: Four paper cups, drawing pin, tape, pin, pen tube, two pieces of wood, wire, shoebox, cotton, clay.

drawing pin and sticky tape. Push a pin through the tiny hole in the side of the tube, and place it on the wire upright, so that it pivots easily on the pin. Now take the anemometer to a windy place outside, on a table. (*Continued below.*)

Drawing pin

Pin in ventilation hole on side of pen case

Wooden cross pieces taped and pinned to pen tube.

Hole in shoebox lid

Empty ballpoint pen tube

Wire upright

Coathanger or similar wire, looped at bottom.

Loop taped into shoebox

Shoebox

Cotton thread

Modelling-clay weight

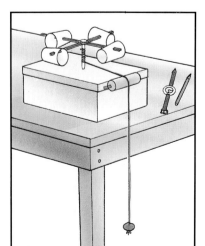

(*Continued from above.*) Tie a length of cotton to the pin in the side of the tube, leading it sideways over a roller (the centre of a kitchen roll). Let it hang down at the side of the table. Fix a small modelling clay weight at the end of the cotton, just touching the ground (*left*). Let the cups go, and they should swing round in the wind. Use a watch to

time how long the clay weight takes to rise from the ground to the edge of the table.

143

Moisture in the Air

The air in the atmosphere is hardly ever dry. It contains **water vapour**, which is the 'gas' form of water. Like other atmospheric gases, water vapour is invisible. But when the vapour turns to liquid (**condenses**) it forms small floating droplets of water, which we see as clouds, mist and fog. When the droplets become too big, they come down as rain.

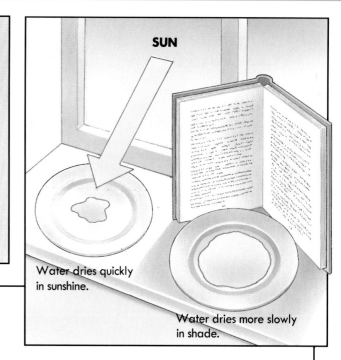

SUN

Water dries quickly in sunshine.

Water dries more slowly in shade.

'Disappearing' Water!

After a rainstorm, there are puddles everywhere. But when the Sun comes out, they soon disappear. Where does the water go? The Sun's warmth turns the liquid water into invisible water vapour, by **evaporation**. (Evaporation is the reverse of condensation.) The water 'dries up'.

Changing liquid water into vaporized water requires energy, usually in the form of heat. When our bodies get very hot, after much exercise, sweat droplets form on our skin. As the water in the droplets evaporates, it draws heat from the body and so we cool down.

You can show that the Sun's heat evaporates water by a simple experiment (*above*). Put two identical saucers on a sunny windowsill, and half-fill each with cold water. Put a 'sunshade' over one, such as a propped-up book.

How it works: Shielded from the Sun's rays, the water in the saucer dries less quickly than the water in full sunshine.

Equipment: Two saucers, water

Evaporating sweat from the skin cools the body when we are too hot.

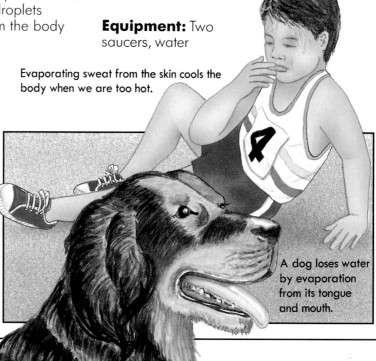

A dog loses water by evaporation from its tongue and mouth.

Where's Foggiest?

Fog and mist are tiny water droplets floating in the air, like clouds at ground level. In a true fog, it is impossible to see clearly for more than 1000 metres (just over 1000 yards). On the Grand Banks, off Canada's Newfoundland, it is sometimes foggy for weeks on end. Here, there are true fogs for an average of one day in three each year.

Humidity – Wet or Dry?

The amount of water vapour in the air is called the humidity. When the humidity is low, sweat evaporates quickly from the body, and our skin feels dry. In high humidity, sweat cannot evaporate easily since the air already carries much water vapour. We say the weather is 'muggy' or 'sticky'.

Humidity level is measured by a psychrometer. This is made from two thermometers: a standard dry-bulb one, and one with wet muslin wrapped around it. Water evaporates from the wet bulb, and so this one registers a lower temperature. The greater the difference between the two readings, the lower the humidity.

▶ A home-made psychrometer needs two thermometers. The wet bulb must be kept very damp all the time for an accurate reading.

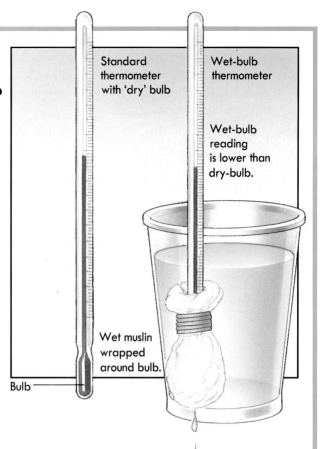

Standard thermometer with 'dry' bulb

Wet-bulb thermometer

Wet-bulb reading is lower than dry-bulb.

Bulb

Wet muslin wrapped around bulb.

Handy Hints for Desert Survival!

Water is continuously evaporating into the air from many places on the Earth's surface, including seas, lakes, rivers, damp soil, wet roofs and roads, and plants and animals. This can be trapped as liquid water by a moisture trap, using the temperature change between day and night.

For people lost in the desert, this small drink could mean the difference between life and death. You do not have to be stranded in the desert, your own garden or park will do, provided you are allowed to dig a hole!

The Moisture Trap

Dig a conical hole and put in it a plastic beaker. In late afternoon, spread over it a plastic sheet, anchor it with large stones and place smaller pebbles in the centre (*right*). Cool air holds less water vapour than warm air. As the temperature falls at night, water vapour in the air and from the soil condenses on the plastic sheet and drips into the beaker.

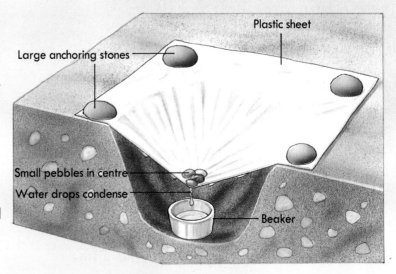

Plastic sheet

Large anchoring stones

Small pebbles in centre

Water drops condense

Beaker

Clouding the View

One of the most obvious features of our weather are the clouds floating across the sky. They are made of billions of water droplets formed from condensed water vapour, or of ice crystals made from frozen water droplets.

There are several main types of cloud, according to their shape and their height above the Earth's surface. For example, cirrus clouds are thin, wispy 'streams' at heights of over 10 kilometres (more than 6 miles). Cumulus clouds have flat bases and billowing, cotton-wool tops. Experts can predict the weather from the cloud types and the speed at which they move, blown by the wind. Cumulus may bring showers, while Nimbus means long periods of rain.

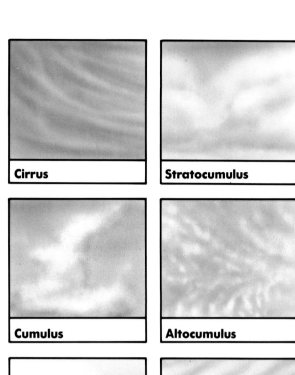

Cirrus

Stratocumulus

Cumulus

Altocumulus

Stratus

Nimbus

▲ 'Smog' is a combination of smoke and fog. It forms where air is polluted with vehicle exhaust fumes. There is a complicated chemical reaction between the fumes and the air, in the presence of sunlight. This smog-bound city is Santiago, in Chile. Smog can be prevented if cars become cleaner.

► Towering cumulonimbus are often called 'storm clouds'. They tend to bring lightning, thunder and heavy rain (see page 152). The dark base is only about 1 kilometre ($\frac{1}{2}$ mile) above the ground. The anvil-shaped spreading top may be over 6 kilometres (4 miles) high.

Cumulonimbus

Clouds in the Bathroom?

Run a warm bath in a cold bathroom and the air soon turns steamy and 'cloudy'. The 'steam' is a mixture of water vapour and tiny water droplets, like the ones that form clouds. It floats up in air which rises because it has been warmed by the hot water in the bathtub. Water vapour condenses on cold surfaces like the windows. These are like dewdrops, which condense from air onto the ground, when a cold night follows a warm day.

See 'Invisible' Dust!

Air is hardly ever perfectly clean. Tiny particles of dust float on the slightest wind. This is important, because each water droplet or ice crystal, in a cloud or fog, needs a tiny particle around which it can form and grow. It may be a piece of solid matter from dust or smoke, or salt from seaspray, or even chemicals from vehicle exhausts and factory fumes. You can see the 'invisible' dust in air by almost closing the curtains on a very sunny day.

How it works: Tiny pieces of dust glint in the narrow shaft of sunlight.

Particles of dust reflect sunlight. _____

The Water Cycle

The Earth always has about the same amount of water. This water is always on the move, in a never-ending cycle. The water cycle produces the most noticeable parts of our weather – clouds, fog, rain and snow.

Water vapour in the atmosphere condenses to form clouds and fog. Water falls to the surface as rain, and also frozen as hail and snow (see page 150). This 'fallen water' travels around on the surface. It filters through the soil, and runs in streams and rivers to the sea. Meanwhile, water is passing from the surface back into the air, as it evaporates to form water vapour. This 'risen water' also travels around in the atmosphere, carried as clouds and invisible water vapour blown by the wind.

▶ Water changes from vapour, to liquid, to solid and back again. The entire cycle is driven by heat energy from the Sun.

How Much Rain Have We Had?

You can record rainfall by making a simple rain gauge. Choose an open area such as a lawn, which is not shielded from the rain.

Bury a large jar with its neck at ground level. Carefully cut a small hole in the centre of a square sheet of stiff plastic (like the plastic packaging around toys). Choose a plastic funnel with the same diameter as the jar, cutting its top down if necessary. Jam its spout into the hole and put the sheet over the jar (right).

Each day, lift out the jar and measure the depth of rain water inside. This is how much rain has fallen since the last reading. Always tip away the water before replacing the jar!

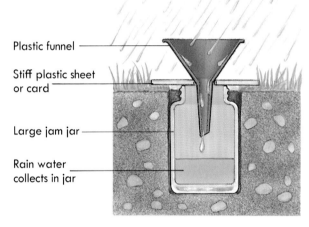

Plastic funnel

Stiff plastic sheet or card

Large jam jar

Rain water collects in jar

Where is Wettest?

Rainfall is measured in millimetres (or inches) per year. The world's wettest place is Tutunendo, in Colombia, South America. Its average is 11,770 mm (463 inches) of rain each year! The average rainfall in London, England, is a mere 585 mm (24 inches)!

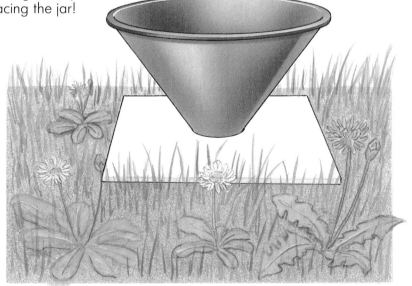

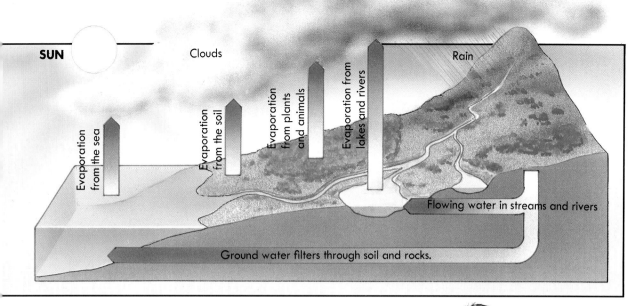

SUN   Clouds   Rain

Evaporation from the sea

Evaporation from the soil

Evaporation from plants and animals

Evaporation from lakes and rivers

Flowing water in streams and rivers

Ground water filters through soil and rocks.

From Raindrops to Dry Puddles

Here are two simple experiments to study rain. Find an area where a puddle always forms after rain, such as on paving stones or tarmac. When the rain stops, draw a line around the puddle's edge with a piece of chalk. Then draw another line each hour afterwards, to measure how fast the puddle dries out (*right*). Try the experiment in different kinds of weather. You can probably guess that the puddle will dry faster if the Sun shines. But what about wind? Does the puddle disappear faster on a calm day or a windy one?

You can also compare the number and size of raindrops. Carefully cut a large sheet of plain, absorbent paper, such as the

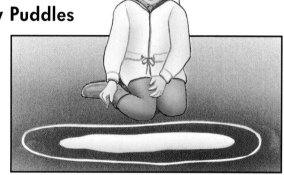

Chalk line marks edge of puddle 1 hour ago.

back of a spare length of wallpaper. Put the paper out in light drizzle for a certain time, such as five seconds. Quickly draw around the wet spots caused by the raindrops (*below*). Compare the result with the spots from a heavy shower.

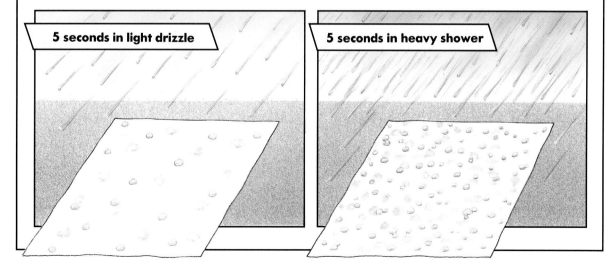

5 seconds in light drizzle

5 seconds in heavy shower

Rain, Hail and Snow

Water moves from the atmosphere to the Earth's surface in many forms, including rain, hail, snow, frost and dew. Sometimes the water goes straight back to the atmosphere. For example, a light snowfall may melt as soon as the Sun comes out, and the water evaporates back in the air. Or snow might fall in a very cold place, such as Antarctica, and be covered by more snow. Over time it is compressed into ice, and stays there for thousands of years. Both these journeys are part of the water cycle.

Raindrops usually form as ice crystals in a cloud, but they melt as they fall. Snowflakes form in the same way, but stay frozen if the air temperature is at or below freezing point (0°C, 32°F). Hailstones are raindrops that move back up into the cloud on rising air currents, and freeze into solid balls of ice.

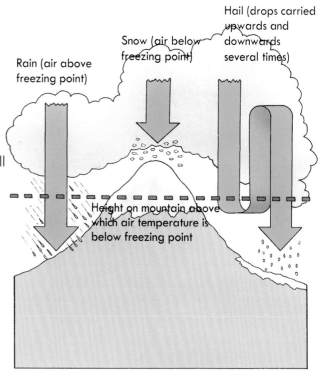

Rain (air above freezing point)

Snow (air below freezing point)

Hail (drops carried upwards and downwards several times)

Height on mountain above which air temperature is below freezing point

Rain

Snow

Hail

Biggest Hailstones

Most hailstones are pea-sized, but occasionally are large. A huge hailstone fell on Kansas, USA, in 1970. It measured 19 centimetres (7 inches) across and weighed 750 grams (1·6 pounds). Bigger ones have fallen, but no one has measured them before they melted!

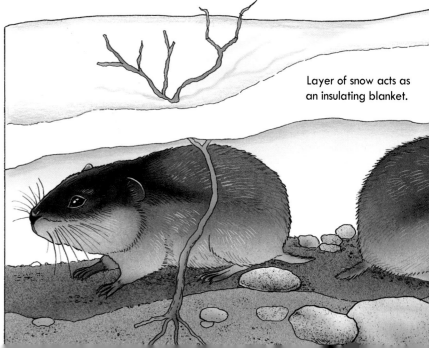

Layer of snow acts as an insulating blanket.

150

Be Jack Frost: Make a Pattern on a Plate!

Equipment: Petroleum jelly, glass plate.

At night, water vapour condenses from the air and normally forms dewdrops. If the surface temperature is below freezing, the water freezes into ice crystals, which we call frost.

To make a frost pattern smear a little make-up cream or petroleum jelly on your finger, and draw a design on a clean glass plate. Put the plate in a freezer next to a plastic beaker of warm water. The water vapour condenses and freezes on the clean parts of the plate, but not on the greasy parts. After an hour or two, your pattern is revealed!

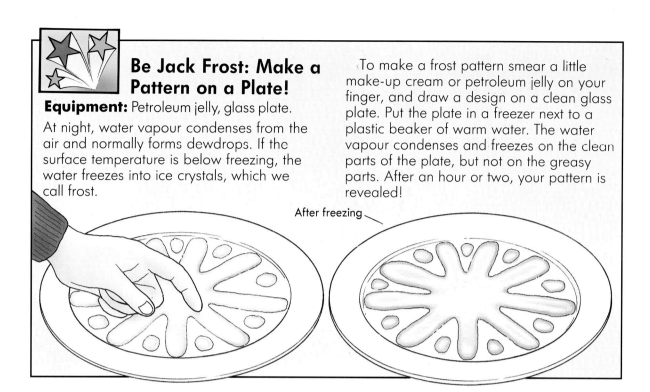

After freezing

Snug under the Snow

Snow may feel icy to us but in very cold places, such as the Arctic, a covering of snow acts like a blanket, that helps many creatures and plants to keep relatively warm. Above the snow, in the icy blasts of winter wind, the air temperature may fall to minus 4°C (about minus 40°F) or even lower. But the layer of loose snow holds tiny pockets of trapped air, just like a feather duvet. Air is a good insulator. Under their blanket of snow, creatures like lemmings and voles dig tunnels and continue to feed through the coldest weather. The temperature in the tunnels is only just below freezing – but that is much warmer than above the snow!

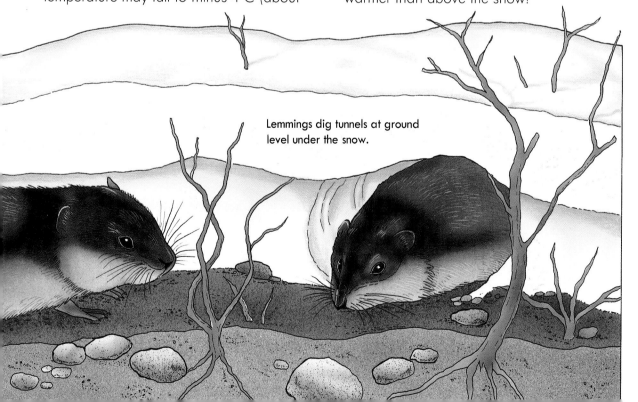

Lemmings dig tunnels at ground level under the snow.

Light and Sound

The weather can veer from one extreme to another in minutes. In a thunderstorm, deafening claps of thunder shake the ground and bolts of lightning split the dark sky. This is weather at its most powerful and violent. Yet soon after, the thunderclouds roll away, the wind drops, the Sun comes out, and a rainbow arches across the sky.

▲ The cactus desert of Arizona, USA, is lit up by jagged bolts of lightning known as 'fork lightning'. If the flash is far away, or spread out through the clouds, it is 'sheet lightning'.

Make Your Own Lightning!

Equipment: A large iron or steel saucepan (not aluminium) with a plastic handle, a rubber glove, an iron or steel fork, and a waste-bin liner.

You can make a tiny, harmless version of a lightning flash at home. Tape a plastic sheet to a table top. Hold a large iron saucepan by its insulating handle, with a rubber glove on that hand, and rub the pan vigorously to and fro on the plastic sheet. This gives the pan an electrical charge (see opposite). Then, holding a fork firmly in the other hand, bring its prongs slowly near to the saucepan's rim. When the gap between pan and fork is small, a tiny spark should jump across. (It may help to darken the room by drawing the curtains, to see the spark more clearly.) It is as though the pan is the 'thundercloud', the fork is the 'lightning conductor' (see opposite), and you are the 'Earth's surface'.

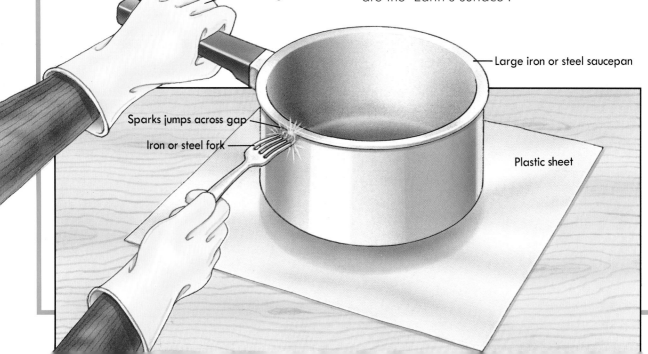

Rubber glove

Sparks jumps across gap

Iron or steel fork

Large iron or steel saucepan

Plastic sheet

How Far Away is Thunder?

In a thundercloud, small ice crystals, with positive electrical charges, float up near the top of the cloud. Larger ones, with negative charges, stay near the bottom. This separation of electrical charges is very unstable, and lightning is the way the charges are equalized again. The first part of the flash, the 'lead stroke', carries negative electricity down towards the ground. It is met by the 'return stroke' bringing positive charges up from the ground. The intensely hot lightning bolt heats the air around it, which suddenly expands, making the noise of thunder.

► Lightning and thunder are created together, but light travels faster than sound. Count the seconds between flash and clap, divide by 3. This is the storm's distance in kilometres.

▲ A jumbo-jet in storm clouds is lit by nearby lightning flashes. If lightning should strike, it spreads harmlessly over the aircraft, although it may disturb the flight instruments.

Lightning Conductors

Lightning flashes do not always reach the ground. If they do, they head for tall objects sticking up from the surface, such as big trees or buildings. If lightning strikes a tree, the tree may burst into flames. Lightning conductors prevent damage to tall buildings. These large strips of metal run between the topmost point and the ground. They give the lightning's energy a harmless route into the Earth.

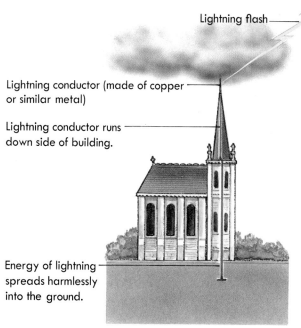

Lightning flash

Lightning conductor (made of copper or similar metal)

Lightning conductor runs down side of building.

Energy of lightning spreads harmlessly into the ground.

All the Colours of . . .

A rainbow is one of the most surprising, beautiful yet fleeting parts of the weather. It is caused by the Sun shining on raindrops. Each drop of water acts as a tiny prism (see *opposite*) and splits the almost-white sunlight into its separate colours (see *below*). On a bright sunny day, you can make your own small rainbow with a hosepipe. Turn on the water for a powerful flow. Place your thumb over the end of the pipe to scatter the water into thousands of tiny drops.

How it works: As the drops fall through the air, they act like rain and make a rainbow.

▶To see the rainbow, you must stand with your back to the Sun. The 'rain-bow' is in fact a 'rain-circle'. You can only see part of it from the ground. People in an aeroplane can see the whole circle.

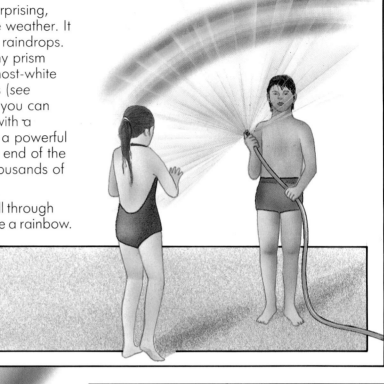

ROYGBIV

Sunlight is a mixture of different colours of light, which the rainbow shows as separate. The main seven colours are always in the same order. Red is on the outside of the arc, then Orange, Yellow, Green, Blue, Indigo, and Violet inside. Remember this by the historical saying: 'Richard Of York Gained Battles In Vain.'

The Heat Haze

On a hot day you might see a 'heat haze'. The Sun heats up the ground more quickly than the air. The hot ground warms the air just above it, which then rises, carrying dust and other small particles. The rising air and dust interfere with light waves, bending them as they pass through, to produce the shimmering effect. A dark road is a good place to look, since the dull tarmac surface heats up as well (see *page 133*).

... The Rainbow!

Equipment: White card, mirror, bowl.

A **prism** is a transparent object with angled sides that bends the different colours in white light by different amounts. You can split sunlight to form a 'long flat rainbow' by making a 'long flat raindrop'.

Choose an open window in direct sunlight. Almost fill a bowl with clean water. Prop a piece of white card upright, next to the bowl. Hold a mirror in the water (*right*).

How it works: The curved water surface, where the water meets the glass, makes a prism that separates the colours in sunlight.

▼ The bright Sun can, in hot places, produce heat hazes and even mirages. In a mirage, light rays from the sky reflect off the layer of very hot air near the ground, and then up into your eyes. It is like looking into a mirror and seeing a reflection of the sky. Because the image is blue and wavy with heat haze, it looks like water.

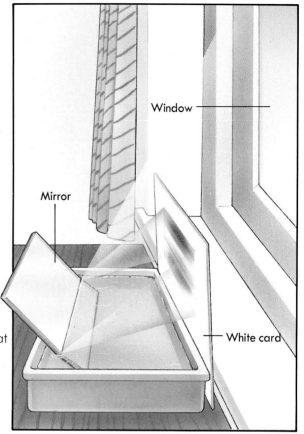

Window

Mirror

White card

Weather Forecasts

Weather affects us all. On a sunny day, we can go outside. If it is raining, we'll probably stay indoors. Farmers plant their crops when the soil is moist, and harvest them when the weather is dry. If we know what the weather is likely to be we can make better plans. A whole branch of science, **meteorology**, is devoted to the study of weather.

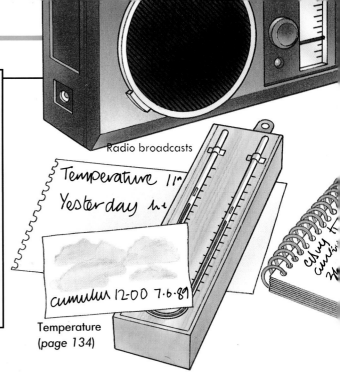

Radio broadcasts

Temperature
(page 134)

Your Own Weather Station

The various projects in this book show you how to build your own weather-measuring instruments and make weather records. On the right, you can see how to make a wind-strength recorder. It measures wind speed and direction at different heights above the ground (see also page 143). You can combine all your results in a Weather Notebook, along with information from the newspapers, radio and television. Include atmospheric pressure readings (see page 158) from a **barometer**. Look for patterns in the weather. For example, does a sudden fall in temperature and an increase in wind speed mean rain is more likely?

Gathering the Information

Weather experts, or meteorologists, collect information from many sources, as shown here. They also obtain measurements from other countries, as part of the worldwide weather-recording network. The recordings from each place must be made in the same way, so that they can be compared and combined accurately.

The methods and measurements are agreed by the World Meteorological Organization (WMO). For example, wind speed varies with height. So the WMO has set a standard height of 10 metres (33 feet) above the ground, for recording winds. Much of the information is nowadays fed into powerful computers, which can look for patterns in the weather.

Weather stations

Weather balloons

Aeroplane reports

Weather ships

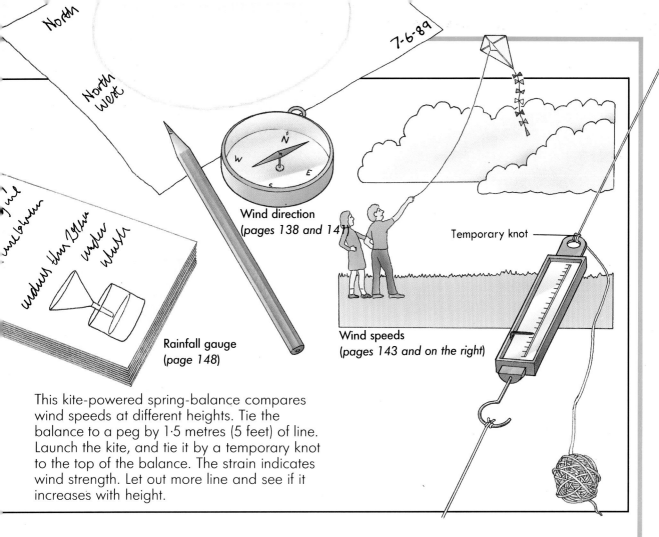

Wind direction
(*pages 138 and 141*)

Rainfall gauge
(*page 148*)

Temporary knot

Wind speeds
(*pages 143 and on the right*)

This kite-powered spring-balance compares wind speeds at different heights. Tie the balance to a peg by 1·5 metres (5 feet) of line. Launch the kite, and tie it by a temporary knot to the top of the balance. The strain indicates wind strength. Let out more line and see if it increases with height.

▶ The control centre of a large meteorological centre is packed with computers, display screens and weather maps. Accurate forecasting of a big storm could save lives.

▶ A network of weather satellites, such as METEOSAT, send information down to ground stations.

Weather satellites

Weather aircraft

The Weather Map

Every day, the experts make weather forecasts that are given in the newspapers and on radio and television. Some people, like farmers and pilots listen to them regularly and are familiar with the special weather-words such as '**front**' and '**low**'.

One of the clearest ways of showing what the weather is doing is to draw a weather map. But what do all the lines, squiggles, numbers and arrows mean? Some of the main ones are described below. As you become more familiar with the words and symbols you can use your own weather observations to predict changes in the weather.

High pressure
The atmospheric air pressure (see *page 132*) varies with time, and from place to place. If it is higher than normal, this is called an area of high pressure or 'high'.

Low pressure
Places with lower than average atmospheric pressure are 'lows'. Pressure is measured in millibars (mbs). Standard atmospheric pressure at sea level is 1,013 mbs.

Isobar
On a map, contour lines join places of equal height above sea level. The lines (isobars) on the weather map join areas of equal atmospheric pressure.

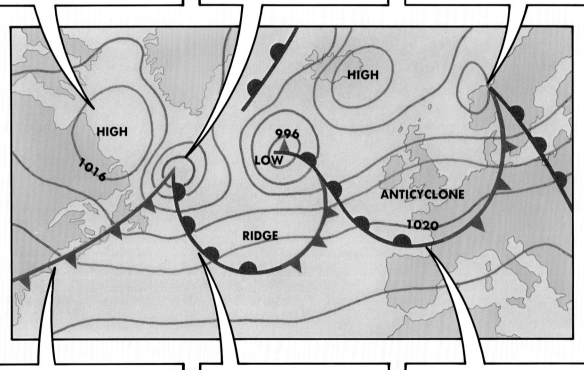

Cold front
Here a region of cold air is moving against a region of warm air. The cold air, being denser, pushes under the warm air and makes it rise, and rain falls.

Warm front
This mass of warm air is pushing up against a region of cold air. The warm air is lighter and rises. Its water vapour condenses, forming clouds and rain.

Anticyclone
This is an area of high pressure, around which winds blow (see *opposite*). It often brings settled, fine weather. In winter the clear skies may mean frost.

The High Pressure System

'Highs', or anticyclones, take up vast areas of the Earth's atmosphere and affect the weather across whole continents. The 'high' is a region of high atmospheric pressure in which cool air sinks to the ground and then spreads out in the form of circling winds. The whole system may be thousands of kilometres across and 10 kilometres (over 6 miles) in height.

In the Northern Hemisphere (the northern half of the world, above the Equator) the winds blow in a clockwise direction. In the Southern Hemisphere, they blow anti-clockwise. This is a result of the forces generated by the spinning Earth, in what is called the Coriolis Effect.

▶ The sinking air in the centre of a 'high' usually means clear skies, sunshine and generally fine weather. This diagram shows a high pressure system in the Northern Hemisphere, where the winds spiral outwards in a clockwise direction.

Cool air
sinks towards ground

Area of high pressure
in centre

Winds blow outwards and clockwise (in Northern
Hemisphere).

The Low Pressure System

The 'low', also called a 'depression' or cyclone, is almost the reverse of the 'high'. Winds spiral inwards, in an anti-clockwise direction in the Northern Hemisphere, and clockwise in the Southern Hemisphere. The air in the centre rises, cooling as it does so. Cyclones in tropical areas may develop into hurricanes. Outside the tropics, they usually mean unsettled, wet, windy weather.

A typical 'low' is 2000 kilometres (1250 miles) across and up to 12 kilometres (7·5 miles) in height. Cyclones tend to move and change faster than anticyclones. They are born, then grow and mature, and finally fade away and die, in some cases within a few days.

▶ As air rises in a cyclone, it cools in the upper atmosphere to form clouds, and often rain. Western Europe, and especially the British Isles, are often affected by cyclones moving eastwards from the Atlantic Ocean, bringing strong winds and wet, blustery weather.

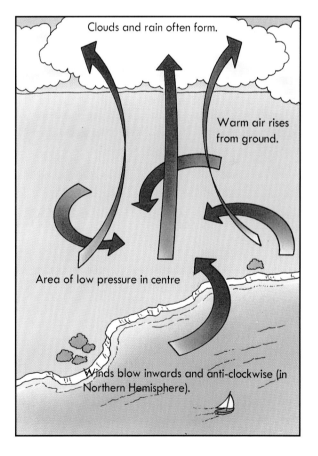

Clouds and rain often form.

Warm air rises
from ground.

Area of low pressure in centre

Winds blow inwards and anti-clockwise (in
Northern Hemisphere).

Weather Power

Every day, the land is under attack from the weather. Rocks are cracked by the Sun and by ice. Rain washes away loose soil. Rivers and glaciers rub great channels deep into the surface. The wind whips up waves that crash against the shoreline. These processes, known together as **weathering**, continually re-shape the landscape.

Make Your Own River!

Rivers are surface grooves along which water flows downhill. You can show how running water has the power to wear away, or erode, its banks. Place a layer of damp sand or soil on a large board, making a few 'hills' and 'valleys' in the landscape. Prop up one end of the board to make a shallow slope. Very slowly, trickle water from a jug onto the middle of the upper side. The water soon finds the quickest path down the slope. As it wears away a main channel, it carries away particles of sand or soil. This is erosion in action. (It is also why you should do this project outside!)

Water cuts away a 'cliff' on the outside of each bend.

A New Course

Over hundreds and thousands of years, huge land movements buckle and tilt the Earth's surface. Copy this by tilting the board slightly, to see how your 'river' finds a new course.

Equipment: Sand, board, water.

Trickle of water from jug

Board

Old river course before tilting

Sand or soil landscape

River

Sculpted in Stone

Over thousands of years, the forces of the weather can reduce the hardest of stone to dust. But the Earth's surface is made of many different rocks, some tougher than others. The softer rocks are worn away faster, leaving the hard ones. In the USA's Monument Valley, Arizona, hot sunshine and sand-blasting winds have rubbed away the softer rock to reveal harder 'stumps' of stone. To the west, the Colorado River (*left*) has cut the gigantic Grand Canyon deep into the Earth.

The Power of Ice

Water, like air, becomes more dense and contracts as it cools (*see page 133*). But when its temperature goes below 4°C (about 39°F), it begins to expand again and get bigger. As the water freezes into ice it continues to expand – and almost nothing can stop it.

Ice that forms in plumbing pipes may split them open. When the temperature rises and a thaw sets in, the ice melts, and the water floods out! This is why, in cold weather, it is important to wrap (lag) water pipes and protect them from the freezing temperatures.

▼ Fill an empty plastic ice-cream or margarine container with water, right to the brim. Clip on the lid, and place it in a freezer or icebox. As the water freezes into ice, it expands and pushes off the lid.

After freezing, the lid is pushed off by ice power.

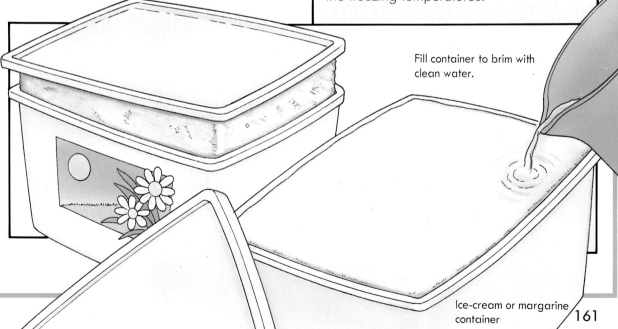

Fill container to brim with clean water.

Ice-cream or margarine container

Weather and Climate

Weather shapes the physical world of rocks and running water. It also affects the living world – the types of plants and animals in each area. However, the word 'weather' applies to conditions in a small area, such as a county or state, and over a short time, during days or weeks. The word **climate** is used for whole countries and continents, and during long time periods, from years to many centuries. The world can be divided into several 'climate zones' (see page 165). In the tropics around the Equator, the climate is warm all year round, and daylight is very nearly 12 hours each day. At the North and South Poles, it is bitterly cold, and there is continuous daylight for half the year and darkness for the other half.

Climate zones going up a mountain are similar to those going 'up the world' from the tropics to the North Pole (see page 165). Mountain zones are narrower. Temperatures fall by 1°C for every 155 metres (1°F for every 280 feet) above sea level.

Mountain Climate Zones

1 Permanent ice and snow on the summit.
2 Alpine scrub, with cold winters and short summers.
3 Montane forest, often damp from cloud and rain.
4 Tropical forests need both high temperature and rainfall.
5 Tropical grasslands form in warm but drier regions.

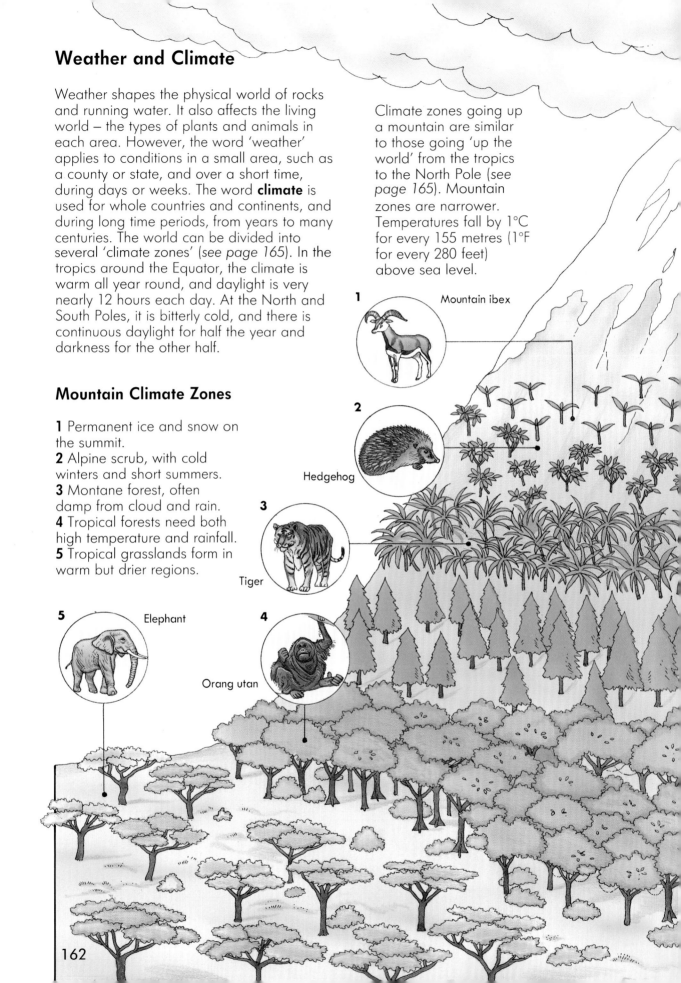

1 Mountain ibex

2 Hedgehog

3 Tiger

4 Orang utan

5 Elephant

Houses Against the Weather

Probably the most widespread animal in the world is the human. People can live almost anywhere, from the tropics to the poles, because they build dwellings that shield them from the weather. The dwellings differ from one region to another, depending on local conditions such as the temperature, rainfall and wind, and also the local building materials. In addition, history and tradition shape our houses.

In the pine forests of the cold, snowy north, there are plenty of trees available. A common design is the log cabin (*right, above*). Its thick walls keep wind and snow out, and keep heat in.

The Tuaregs of the Sahara build tents of thin poles and animal skins (*right, middle*). The wide roof gives good shade, and open doors allow a cooling breeze. A 'typical English cottage' (*right, bottom*) has a roof thatched from locally grown reeds, small windows, and timber-framed or stone walls. It is cool in summer and warm in winter.

Log cabin

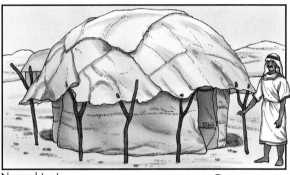
Nomad tent

Thatched cottage

How a house's heat is lost

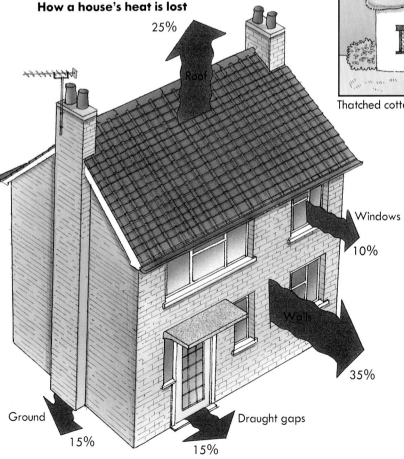

25%
Roof

Windows
10%

Walls
35%

Ground
15%

Draught gaps
15%

Today's Typical House

Many modern houses have been built to a standard square-box design. This makes a house easier and cheaper to build, but means that traditional dwellings with 'local character' are disappearing.

◀ In the past few years, we have realized that it is vital to save energy, especially from 'fossil fuels' such as coal, oil and gas. A typical house loses heat energy in many ways (*left*). We can cut down the waste by better building methods and materials, along with extra insulation.

Nature and the Weather

In natural wild places, plants and animals live in harmony with the weather and the seasons. With the warmth and moisture of spring, seeds begin to grow. Animals feed on the growing plants and begin to raise their young. In summer, the plants flower. Bees, birds and other creatures spread the flower pollen, helping to form seeds. In autumn the seeds and fruits ripen, while animals feed well and make stores for the winter. In winter many plants and animals go to 'sleep' until spring.

Gardeners must look after plants, weeding and watering, protecting them from animals, and perhaps raising them in a greenhouse. Left on their own, these 'unnatural' plants usually die, and the natural plants and animals take over.

Seaweed   Fir cone

Many plants use the weather, and especially the wind, to spread their seeds. Dandelion and thistle 'parachutes' float on the slightest breeze. Ash seeds, or 'keys', twirl away from the tall parent tree on their 'wings'. The wind shakes the seeds from ripe poppy capsules. As lupin pods dry out they suddenly snap open and fling their seeds away. A piece of seaweed absorbs moisture from humid air and becomes flexible and rubbery rather than stiff and dry. Fir cones open their scales in dry weather, to release the seeds within.

Dandelion seeds

Ash seeds

Thistle seeds

Lupin seeds

Poppy seeds

Weather Folklore

Many local sayings and legends are based on the weather. In Britain, 15 July is St Swithin's Day. It is said that if it rains on this day, it will rain for 40 days. Statistics show that the myth is not really true. In the USA, 2 February is Groundhog Day. It is said that the groundhog wakes up from winter sleep and looks outside its burrow. If it sees its own shadow, the weather is fine – but cold, so the groundhog goes back to sleep for six more weeks.

Animals Around the World

Wild creatures of the world cannot live anywhere. A gorilla could not survive in the icy wastes of Antarctica. An Arctic hare would not live long in a tropical forest. Each kind of animal is suited only to a certain climate. The climate has direct effects on the animal itself, by its temperature, humidity, rainfall and winds. It also has effects on the surrounding animals and plants, which provide food and shelter for others, and which are all tied into the natural network of life.

The broad wildlife zones across the world are known as 'biomes', and they resemble the different zones as you travel up a mountain (see page 162). However, some animals have been able to 'cheat' nature and spread to unsuitable areas – but only with our help. Farm animals such as sheep, cattle, goats and pigs are fed and housed by us, in places where they could not otherwise survive. Cats, dogs and other pets rely on us for food and shelter. More unwelcome guests like rats and mice survive almost anywhere that we do.

▼ The diagram below shows the main climate zones from the Equator to the North Pole, and examples of animals from each zone. There are similar zones towards the South Pole.

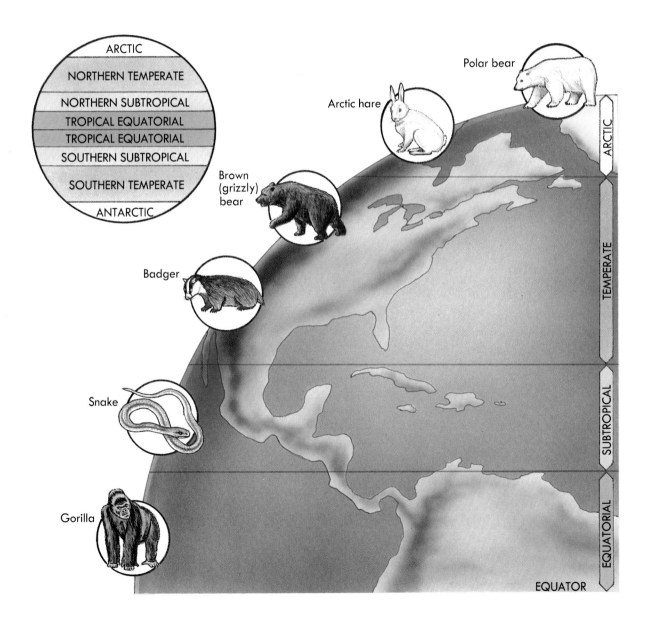

ARCTIC
NORTHERN TEMPERATE
NORTHERN SUBTROPICAL
TROPICAL EQUATORIAL
TROPICAL EQUATORIAL
SOUTHERN SUBTROPICAL
SOUTHERN TEMPERATE
ANTARCTIC

Polar bear

Arctic hare

Brown (grizzly) bear

Badger

Snake

Gorilla

ARCTIC

TEMPERATE

SUBTROPICAL

EQUATORIAL

EQUATOR

A Change in the Weather?

The Earth's climate has changed many times in the past. Subtropical forests have spread from the south into temperate areas. Millions of years later, ice sheets have spread from the north. Today, the great danger is that we are changing the climate. Can Earth survive?

The Greenhouse Effect

In bright sunshine, the air inside a greenhouse becomes warm. The greenhouse glass lets in the Sun's light energy and some of its heat energy. Inside, part of this energy is 'reflected' and converted into a different type, which cannot pass back out through the glass so easily. The energy, in the form of heat, builds up inside the greenhouse.

You can show this with two identical glass jars, each containing cold water. Wrap one in a plastic bag (this is the greenhouse 'glass'). Leave them in the Sun for an hour. Then measure the temperature of the water in each jar (above). Which is warmer?

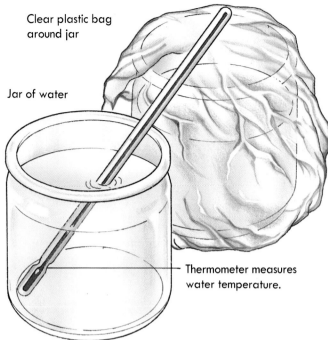

Clear plastic bag around jar

Jar of water

Thermometer measures water temperature.

Equipment: Thermometer, glass jar, plastic bag.

The same thing is now happening to the Earth. Over the past few centuries, people have been burning fuels such as wood, coal, oil, gas and petrol, in ever-increasing amounts. The gases formed by the burning, such as carbon dioxide, are building up in the atmosphere. They act like greenhouse glass. The result: experts believe the Earth will heat up and undergo '**global warming**'.

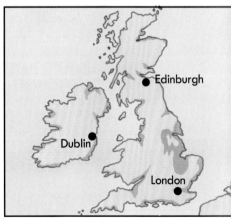

Edinburgh

Dublin

London

◀ ▲ Burning large areas of forest speeds the Greenhouse Effect. As the Earth warms, the oceans will expand and polar icecaps will melt. The rise in sea level could flood many major cities (*above*).

Acid Rain

The weather can transport pollution across seas and continents. Power stations (*right*), factory chimneys and vehicle exhausts pour all manner of chemicals into the atmosphere. They include sulphur dioxide and nitrous oxides. These react with substances already in the atmosphere, and with water, to form weak acids. The polluted clouds and air float for hundreds of kilometres on the wind.

Eventually the acidic moisture falls to Earth as rain – acid rain. The acids damage trees,

▲ Power stations are one of the main sources of fumes that make acid rain.

rivers and lakes, killing fish and other water creatures. They even eat away statues and the stonework of buildings.

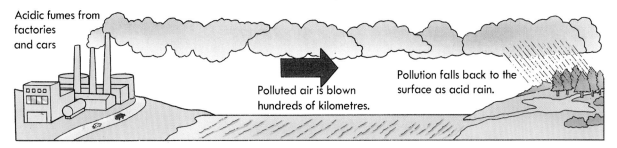

Acidic fumes from factories and cars

Polluted air is blown hundreds of kilometres.

Pollution falls back to the surface as acid rain.

The Ozone Hole, and How We Can All Help

Many of today's products could alter our climate in the future. Recently, experts discovered that certain chemicals in aerosols and fridge cooling fluids are entering the atmosphere and damaging the **ozone layer**. This layer of ozone gas, high in the atmosphere, filters out much of the

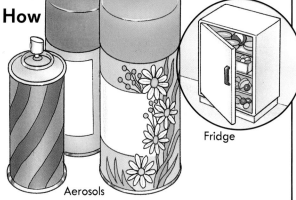

Fridge

Aerosols

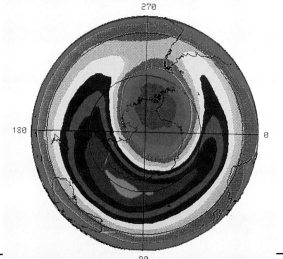

Sun's harmful rays. If the layer becomes thinner or disappears, damaging rays would reach the surface. They could cause many problems, such as an increase in skin cancers.

Manufacturers are now making 'ozone-friendly' aerosols to help reduce the risks.

◀ This computer-coloured satellite photo shows the thinning of the ozone layer over Antarctica, in late 1988 The developing 'hole' is coloured in blue.

Weather Quiz

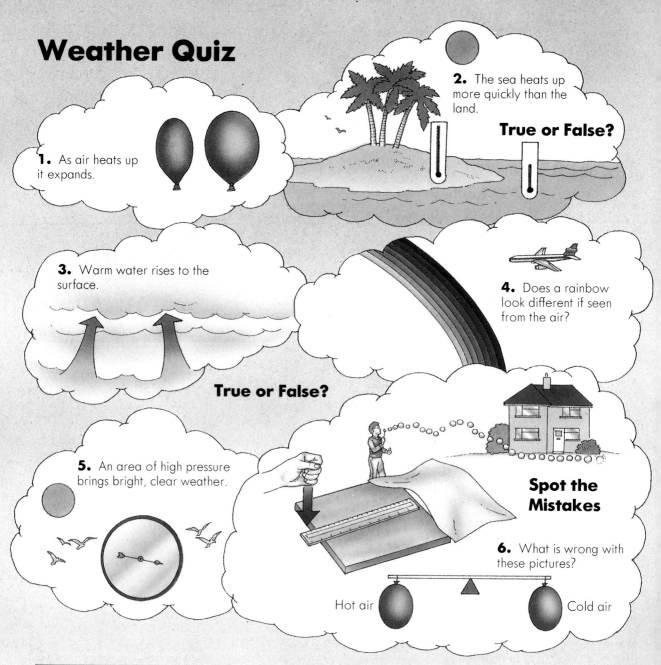

1. As air heats up it expands.

2. The sea heats up more quickly than the land.

True or False?

3. Warm water rises to the surface.

4. Does a rainbow look different if seen from the air?

True or False?

5. An area of high pressure brings bright, clear weather.

Spot the Mistakes

6. What is wrong with these pictures?

Hot air   Cold air

Answers

1. True. All gases expand when they are heated (page 133).

2. False. Water takes longer to heat up than soil so the land will heat up quicker (page 161).

3. True. Warm water rises to the surface, so the ocean depths are colder than the surface. This is also because the Sun's rays do not penetrate far into water (page 139).

4. Yes. A rainbow appears as a circle when viewed from an aeroplane (page 154).

5. True. High pressure does bring good weather (page 159).

6. Top: The bubbles will be carried upwards by the air currents around the house (page 141).
Middle: The air pressure keeps the paper flattened against the table (page 132).
Bottom: Warm air is lighter than cold air so the balloons will not balance as shown (page 133).

168

Glossary

Acid A sour-tasting, corrosive substance that turns the indicator litmus to red.

Acoustics The study of sounds and their qualities. For example, it involves studying how the shape of a room and the materials on the walls affect the quality of sound, as from a hi-fi system.

Anemometer A device for measuring how fast the wind blows.

Atmosphere The 'blanket' of air around the Earth, that is densest near the ground and fades away to nothing in space.

Atom The smallest particle of a substance that still has the chemical and physical properties of that substance.

Barometer A device that measures atmospheric pressure, usually in units called millibars.

Base In chemistry, a bitter-tasting, often slimy substance that turns the indicator litmus to blue.

Battery A device that creates electricity from chemical reactions. A typical torch battery is called a dry cell.

Celsius A unit of measurement for temperature. Water freezes at 0°C (zero degrees Celsius) and boils at 100°C.

Circuit A complete loop or circle made from materials that conduct electricity, such as wires and bulbs. The electricity flows round and round the circuit.

Cloud A collection of billions of tiny water droplets floating in the atmosphere.

Cochlea A small snail-shaped organ deep inside the ear, that converts the vibrations of sounds into electrical nerve signals.

Condensation When a substance changes state from a gas to a liquid.

Conductor A material that lets electricity flow through it, the opposite of an insulator.

Decibel A unit of measurement for the energy in sound waves, which corresponds to its volume or loudness.

Dissolving When a solid chemical 'disappears' into a liquid one, by splitting into invisibly small particles

Doldrums A region around the Equator where winds seldom blow, and so the weather is usually calm.

Dynamo A device that creates electricity by turning round a magnet near a coil of wire.

Eardrum A small flap of skin inside the ear, that vibrates as sounds hit it. The eardrum passes the vibrations to the inner parts of the ear.

Echolocation Detecting the direction and distance of objects by the echoes of sound waves that bounce off them.

Electric current Electricity that flows through a wire, in the same way that water flows through a hose, unlike static electricity.

Electrolysis Splitting a substance into the separate chemicals that make it up, by passing an electric current through it.

Element A basic chemical substance in which all the atoms are the same, and different from the atoms of any other element.

Emulsion Tiny blobs of one liquid floating in another liquid, such as oil droplets floating in water.

Evaporation When a substance changes from a liquid to a gas.

Fuse A piece of very thin wire fitted into an electrical machine, that melts and makes a gap in the circuit if something goes wrong.

Humidity The amount of water vapour in the air. In very humid air we feel damp and 'sticky'. Air of low humidity feels dry.

Indicator A chemical that turns one colour when added to an acid, and another colour when added to a base.

Insulator A material that does not let electricity flow through it, unlike a conductor.

Isobar On a weather map, a line joining areas of equal atmospheric pressure.

Lightning A powerful flash of electricity between the negative electrical charges in clouds or between a cloud and the ground.

Molecule Two or more atoms joined together.

Percussion instrument A musical instrument that is played by banging, hitting or shaking it, such as a drum.

Rain gauge A device for measuring the amount of rain that has fallen. It is usually marked with a scale in millimetres.

Reaction In chemistry, when two or more chemicals combine to make a new chemical substance.

Resonance When the vibrations of a substance, such as the wood of a violin, correspond to the air vibrations which make the sound.

Reverberation A confusing jumble of noises and echoes that makes a sound 'muddy' and unclear.

Sonic boom The barrier of squashed-up (compressed) air in front of something travelling faster than the speed of sound. It is heard as a clap of thunder as the object goes past.

Static electricity Electricity in the form of charged particles, which are either positive or negative. These stay in the object and do not 'flow' like an electric current.

Stethoscope A funnel-shaped device that collects faint sound waves and passes them along a tube to an earpiece, making them easier to hear.

Solar power Energy from the Sun's light and heat rays, which is usually turned into electricity.

Sound wave Patterns of vibrations of the molecules in the air, that we hear as a sound.

Sundial A device for telling the time, using the Sun to cast a shadow onto a dial.

Transformer A device that changes the voltage of electricity — the 'pressure' which pushes the electricity along the wire.

Turbine A fan-shaped wheel that turns at high speed when steam, water or another substance flows past it.

Vocal cords Flaps of muscle in the throat, that vibrate as air passes over them, to make the sounds of the human voice.

Index

Page numbers in *italics* refer to illustrations, or where illustrations and text occur on the same page.

The publishers would like to thank the following for kindly supplying photographs for this book:

Photographic Acknowledgements

Page 12 Courtesy of Ray Alan; 13 Picturepoint; 18 Science Photo Library; 20 ZEFA; 22 Richard Bryant; 23 N.H.P.A./S. Dalton; 24 ZEFA; 25 ARDEA; 28 NASA; 32 Clive Barda; 37 South American Pictures; 39 ZEFA; 41 ZEFA; 45 Paul Brierley (right) Edison National Historical Site (left); 47 N.H.P.A./S. Kraremann (right) N.H.P.A./ A. Bannister (left); 53 Ontario Science Centre, Toronto; 56 ZEFA; 57 The Mansell Collection (top) ZEFA (bottom); 60 The Mansell Collection; 61 Launch Pad/Science Museum, London; 64 Science Photo Library; 70 Ann Ronan Picture Library; 71 ZEFA; 79 Science Photo Library; 80 PLASTIMO; 83 Science Photo Library; 84 N.H.P.A./I.Pulunin; 85 Elga Ltd (top) Holt Studios (bottom); 86 Science Photo Library (top left) Austin Rover (bottom left) Shell Photographic Library (right); 87 Plessey Semi-Conductors Ltd (left) ZEFA (right); 92 Philips; 93 Science Photo Library; 94 Quadrant Picture Library; 96 Science Photo Library; 97 Mary Evans Picture Library (top left) Supersport (bottom left) Science Photo Library (top & bottom right); 98 ZEFA; 100 Science Photo Library; 103 Spectrum Colour Library (left) Science Photo Library (right); 106 Science Photo Library (top) ZEFA (bottom); 108 Science Library (left top & bottom) BOC (right); 110 ZEFA; 112 Science Photo Library; 115 Science Photo Library; 116 Everyready; 117 ZEFA; 120 Science Photo Library; 124 Science Photo Library; 125 N.H.P.A. (top) Science Photo Library (bottom); 126 Friends of the Earth (top) Greenpeace Communications (bottom); 127 Science Photo Library; 134 J.F.P. Galvin; 135 ZEFA; 137 Allsport/Simon Bruty; 140 ZEFA (top) Science Photo Library (bottom); 141 Frank Lane Picture Agency; 142 Science Photo Library; 146 ZEFA; 152 ZEFA; 153 ZEFA; 155 Science Photo Library; 157 Crown Copyright/Reproduced with the permission of the Controller of Her Majesty's Stationery Office; 160 The Hutchison Library; 166 South American Pictures; 167 ZEFA (top) Science Photo Library (bottom).

Picture Research: Elaine Willis